6583

D0351486

The Reality of St⋯⋯te

Michael Armstrong graduated from the London School of Economics, and is a Fellow of the Institute of Personnel and Development and a Fellow of the Institute of Management Consultants. He spent 12 years in general personnel management in the food and engineering industries followed by 10 years as a management consultant with Coopers & Lybrand, where he headed the personnel consultancy division. From 1976 to 1988 he was Personnel Director of Book Club Associates and since then he has practised as an independent HR consultant. His books include *Personnel and the Bottom Line*, *Management Processes and Functions*, and *Using the HR Consultant*.

Phil Long is a graduate of the University of London, where she majored in Occupational Psychology, and is a Fellow of the Royal Society of Arts. She is currently the Research Manager at the Institute of Personnel and Development. Her previous publications include *Retirement – Planned Liberation?*, *The Personnel Professionals*, *Performance Appraisal Revisited*, *Cashless Pay and Deductions* (co-authored with Erich Suter) and *Special Leave* (co-authored with Margaret Hill).

The Reality of
Strategic HRM

Michael Armstrong

and

Phil Long

INSTITUTE OF PERSONNEL
AND DEVELOPMENT

Typesetting by The Comp-Room, Aylesbury
Printed in Great Britain by
Short Run Press, Exeter

British Library Cataloguing in Publication Data
A catalogue record for this book is available from the
British Library

ISBN 0-85292-563-8

**INSTITUTE OF PERSONNEL
AND DEVELOPMENT**

IPD House, Camp Road, London SW19 4UX
Tel: 0181 946 9100   Fax: 0181 947 2570
Registered office as above. Registered Charity No. 1038333
A company limited by guarantee. Registered in England No. 2931892

 **Contents**

Acknowledgements

We would like to acknowledge the considerable help given to us by the chief executives, managing directors and other directors who spared their valuable time to assist us with this research. We could not have done without the frank and fascinating contributions they made to our understanding of what organisations are actually doing about strategic HRM and adding value through people.

We would also like to thank the members of our Steering Group for their help and advice. These consisted of:

Ewart Wooldridge, Director of Resources, The South Bank Centre and Vice President, Employee Relations, Institute of Personnel and Development (Chair).

Vince Harris, Group Personnel Manager, The GEC Co PLC

Professor David Guest, Department of Organisational Psychology, Birkbeck College, University of London

Dr Riccardo Peccei, Department of Industrial Relations, The London School of Economics.

▚ Foreword – by Ewart Wooldridge
Director of Resources, South Bank Centre;
Vice-President (Employee Relations),
Institute of Personnel and Development

Strategic HRM is one of those beguiling terms which belongs too often to the 'retrospective' school of management. It is easier to recognise it *after the event* – when you know a particular change strategy has met the business objectives, united the management team and galvinised the organisation. If we are honest with ourselves, how often can we claim to have planned a strategic HRM approach from the outset and consciously followed it through to a successful outcome?

Much of my career has been involved in managing major change initiatives. That experience has taught me that there is undoubtedly a certain kind of integration between the personnel function and the rest of the management team which can transform the processes that deliver effective change. Michael Armstrong and Phil Long's research, which forms part of the IPD's major research programme on 'Managing People – The *Changing* Frontiers', opens up to close scrutiny the ways in which this integration can happen.

The other vital service performed by this book is to clear the fog away from some very dense concepts of management theory. With the jargon cleared away, we have great clarity of analysis of the factors that pave the way to effective change – strong visionary leadership, well-understood and shared values, a closely-knit top team and the ability to adapt quickly without losing the overall sense of direction.

July 1994

Managing People -
The *Changing* Frontiers

vii

Introduction

The Search for Strategic HRM – from rhetoric to reality

What *is* this thing called strategic HRM? It seems to be part of the brave new world of strategic management and human resource management. But have these terms any real meaning? Do people actually put either strategic management or human resource management into practice? And if they do, what do they look like and what impact, if any, do they make on organisational performance?

As 'managerese', these terms have undoubtedly infiltrated the world of management. They have become part of the everyday vocabulary of many managers – everyone talks about strategies and strategic management, but the words are used loosely and without discrimination. No one seems to agree on exactly what strategy is, or how it is formulated, or what good it is anyway.

The situation is even worse with human resource management, 'HRM' as it is generally known and as it will be called in this book. There has indeed been plenty of rhetoric about HRM. It is interesting to note, however, that it comes almost exclusively from academics. Since HRM was invented in the mid-1980s by the founding fathers (Fombrun et al. in 1984 and Beer et al., also in 1984) there has only been one full article on HRM by a practitioner (Armstrong, 1987) in the leading journal for practitioners in the UK, *Personnel Management*. And the academics, who seem to spend most of their time writing articles either deconstructing the concept of HRM or deconstructing the deconstructions of other academics, do not agree on what HRM is; or if they do agree, do not accept that it has been put into practice; or if they do think it is happening, do not like it.

Many people say that HRM is indistinguishable from personnel management. A large number of personnel specialists, line managers and academics dislike the term because it smacks of manipulation, because they do not think that people should be referred to as 'resources' to be *used* by managements for their own purposes, or even because it originates from the other side of the Atlantic and cannot therefore work here. Some personnel directors have trans-mogrified overnight into human resource directors without any dis-cernible change in their roles, others stick to the old term, denying that the new one has any real meaning.

So when these two somewhat dubious terms are joined together into strategic HRM, has *this* any real meaning? Is it also just rhetoric or is there something in it which provides for added value in the practice of what many people, including ourselves, persist in calling personnel management.

The Personnel Director of a leading British manufacturing com-pany recently denied that there is such a thing as personnel, let alone human resource (HR), strategy. Writers on business strategy, with the exception of Michael Porter (1985), generally ignore the existence of HR strategy as such, although they may refer to 'resource allocation' as a key aspect of business strategy. Two of the leading UK textbooks on the subject (Goold and Campbell, 1986 and Faulkner and Johnson, 1992) do not recognise its existence.

Defining strategic HRM

Many people are in favour of strategic HRM just as they are in favour of virtue. But the concept remains elusive, perhaps because we all have our own definition of what it means and certainly because strategic HRM is practised in many different ways (and why not?) if it is practised at all.

It is not too difficult to produce a definition of strategic HRM along the following lines:

> Strategic human resource management is concerned with the development and implementation of people strategies which are integrated with corporate strategies and ensure that the culture, values and structure of the organisation, and the quality, motivation and commitment of its members contribute fully to the achievement of its goals. (Armstrong, 1991)

But this could easily be dismissed as mere rhetoric – a statement which is full of would-be good intentions but which is meaningless unless it can be demonstrated that it is real in the sense that it has been applied in practice *and* it works.

The search for reality

This book is an attempt to seek the reality of the strategic HRM concept. It is based on:

1. research conducted in 1994 by the writers on behalf of the Institute of Personnel and Development. The research covered ten large and well-known organisations and involved interviews with their personnel/HR directors or, in one case, the head of personnel, and, importantly, in all but two of the organisations, with the chief executive, the finance director and other marketing, operational or planning directors.

    The research covered the following companies which have agreed that their names should be released:

    - Pilkington Optronics
    - Motorola
    - Rover Group.

    The remaining seven organisations preferred to remain anonymous and the pseudonyms used in the text are given below:

    - ABC Distribution, a firm in the food distribution business
    - Albion Bank, a major clearing bank
    - Bookworld, a large publishing firm
    - Loamshire Council, a district council
    - Megastores, one of the UK's leading retailers
    - Morton Healthcare Trust, a large teaching hospital trust
    - Welland Water, a water company.

    The research involved the conduct of 45 extended interviews, 35 of them with chief executives and other financial, marketing and operational directors. The aim of these interviews was to get a cross-section of views about how organisations develop and implement strategies relating to people at the highest level and, importantly, how these 'people' strategies fit in with the business or corporate strategies. We also wanted to get a line management view from the top about strategic HRM and the role of the personnel function. We did not want to rely simply on what we were told by personnel/HR directors.

2. an extensive review of the literature
3. the considerable practical experience of Michael Armstrong as a personnel and strategic planning director

On the basis of this research and experience we decided that it was necessary to explore the meaning of the concept itself. This has to be founded on an analysis of the constituent concepts of strategy, strategic management and HRM and this conceptual framework will be constructed in the first part of the book.

One of the criticisms frequently made of the concept of strategic HRM is that it is based on a misconception of the meaning of strategy and a quite unrealistic and outdated understanding of strategic management. Strategy is conceived as a formal, step-by-step (linear) and analytical process which produces a definitive and fully documented guide to the future as the basis for long-term strategic plans which proceed inexorably towards some well-defined goal and which will enable an equally well-defined mission to be realised. In reality, strategy is not like that at all. As Johnson (1987) has pointed out:

> Strategic decisions are characterized by the political hurly-burly of organizational life with a high incidence of bargaining, a trading off of costs and benefits of one interest group against another, all within a notable lack of clarity in terms of environmental influences and objectives.

Anyone who, like one of the writers, Michael Armstrong, has sat on the board of a business for a number of years and played a full part in strategic business decisions, knows that the process of strategic planning at the top level in an organisation largely works in this way. And if this is generally the case, what is the likelihood of organisations developing written, formal strategic HR plans which have any real meaning and are not exercises in rhetoric?

Not much, the cynics would say, but perhaps this is a wrong basis for defining what strategic HRM is about. Perhaps we should not be looking for highly formalised HR strategies, written down in elaborate detail and dovetailing neatly into equally formalised corporate or business strategies. Perhaps what we *should* be looking for is how organisations manage change in a turbulent, even chaotic environment, and how they develop and define a sense of direction which enables them, their 'ship', and all who sail in her, to negotiate the icebergs without, as it were, simply rearranging the deck chairs. Surely, it is useful to have some idea of the broad direction an organisation might take in an uncertain future. At least, as the cowboys used to say, 'let's keep the herd moving west'.

In the first part, therefore, Chapter 1 explores these issues and aims to answer the questions:

- What is strategy?
- What types of strategies exist and at what levels?
- How are strategies formed – by the top team and by line and specialist managers elsewhere in the organisation?
- How do strategies evolve?
- How are they expressed?
- What is strategic management?

The concept of HRM is equally elusive. David Guest (1989a) has described it as a 'catch-all phrase, reflecting general intentions but devoid of specific meaning'. Although the continuing debate about HRM and personnel management is becoming increasingly sterile, it is not possible to write about strategic HRM without addressing, albeit briefly, the following questions:

- What is HRM as generally conceived?
- In David Guest's (1989b) famous phrase, 'HRM and personnel management: can you tell the difference?'

- To what extent is HRM simply rhetoric?
- If it *is* more than rhetoric, is it a good or a bad thing?

This review takes place in Chapter 2.

These two chapters lead naturally into the third chapter of Part One, which considers the total concept of strategic HRM, how it derives from the concepts of strategy and HRM, and the extent to which strategic HRM can be regarded as a distinctive process of management. This chapter will review the various definitions of strategic HRM, examine the possibilities of strategic integration or fit and discuss the ways in which HR strategies can be developed. A distinction will be made between strategic HRM, as an approach to determining the overall directions to be taken in managing human resources, and HR strategies, which more specifically address particular aspects of the total strategy such as development and resourcing (managing stocks and flows).

Against this background, the aim of the second part of the book is to examine the reality of strategic HRM in terms of what organisations are or are not doing about it. This part will largely be based on our research and will cover:

- the formulation of business and HR strategies (Chapter 4)
- the content of HR strategies (Chapter 6)
- how HR strategies are integrated with corporate/business strategies, how a coherent approach can be achieved and what impact the strategies make on performance

The third and final part of the book will concentrate on the role of the HR function, examining:

- the role of the personnel/HR director in developing and implementing strategy (Chapter 7)
- the contribution the function can make to enhancing added value and achieving sustainable competitive advantage (Chapter 8)
- the methods which can be adopted to evaluate the contribution of the HR function (Chapter 9)
- approaches to developing integrated HR strategies (Chapter 10)

The last part will not attempt to be unduly prescriptive about how HR functions should set about being strategic. It would be unwise to prescribe any particular approach because of the almost infinite variety of circumstances in which HR directors are likely to find themselves. These will be related to the product-market situation of their company and its technology, the rates of growth or change, the external opportunities to be developed or threats to be managed, the political pressures within the organisation and the often conflicting views of its various stakeholders (shareholders, trustees, managers, employees, trade unions and customers). All that can be done, and all that will be attempted in this book, is to illustrate how the case study and other organisations are carrying it out (without any suggestion that what they do represents 'best practice'), to suggest some of the more important points which deserve consideration, and to provide some guidelines on the overall approaches that can be adopted.

Reference will be made to strategic HRM, HRM and HR throughout the book, although it is appreciated that the terms HR/HRM and personnel are often used indiscriminately and are regarded by many practitioners (and the writers of this book) as being virtually interchangeable.

Part One:

The Conceptual Framework

1

The Concept of Strategy

Strategy was, of course, originally a military term, defined in the Oxford English Dictionary as:

> The art of a commander-in-chief; the art of projecting and directing the larger military movements and operations of a campaign.

This may not seem to have much relevance to strategy in business, public sector or voluntary organisations, but at least it conveys the message that strategy is an art and that responsibility for it lies with the head of the organisation.

It was Drucker, inevitably, who as long ago as 1955 pointed out in *The Practice of Management* the importance of strategic decisions, which he defined as 'all decisions on business objectives and on the means to reach them'. However, the concept of business strategy was not fully developed until the three outstanding pioneers, Kenneth Andrews, Igor Ansoff and Alfred Chandler Jr made their mark. They were followed by Michael Porter, Henry Mintzberg and many more who further developed the concepts and adapted them to contemporary conditions.

Strategy defined

Strategy has been defined in various ways by the many writers on this subject, for example:

> Corporate strategy is the pattern of major objectives, purposes or goals and essential policies or plans for reaching these goals, stated in such a way as to define what business the company is in or is to be in, and the kind of company it is or is to be. (Andrews, 1987)

Strategic decisions address the selection of product-market opportunities . . . Strategy and objectives together describe the concept of the firm's business. They specify the amount of growth, the area of growth, the direction for growth, the leading strengths, and the profitability target. (Ansoff, 1987)

Strategy is the determination of the basic long-term goals and objectives of an enterprise, and the adoption of courses of action and the allocation of resources necessary for carrying out these goals. (Chandler, 1962)

Strategy is 'the organization's preselected means or approach to achieving its goals or objectives, while coping with current and future external conditions'. (Digman, 1990)

Strategy is concerned with the long-term direction and scope of an organization. It is also crucially concerned with how the organization positions itself with regard to the environment and in particular to its competitors . . . It is concerned with establishing competitive advantage, ideally sustainable over time, not by technical manoeuvring, but by taking an overall long-term perspective. (Faulkner and Johnson, 1992)

Strategy is the fundamental pattern of present and planned resource deployments and environmental interactions that indicate how the organization will achieve its objectives. (Hofer and Schendel, 1986)

Business strategy is a market-led concept affected by product-market considerations and directed at the achievement of competitive advantage. (Miller, 1991)

Strategy can be defined as

- **a plan** – some sort of consciously intended course of action
- **a pattern** which emerges over time
- **a position** which provides for competitive advantage
- **a perspective** – an abstraction which exists in the minds of people (Mintzberg et al., 1988)

Corporate strategy is what makes the corporate whole add up to more than the sum of its business unit parts. (Porter, 1985)

Strategy is 'the pattern or plan that integrates an organization's major goals, policies and action sequences into a cohesive whole. (Quinn, 1980)

'Strategy is the framework which guides those choices that determine [the organization's] nature and direction.' These choices 'relate to the scope of an organization's products or services, markets, key capabilities, growth, returns and allocation of resources'. (Tregoe and Zimmerman, 1980)

To sum up, strategy may be defined as a statement of what the organisation wants to become, where it wants to go and, broadly, how it means to get there. In its crudest form, strategy in a commercial enterprise answers the questions: 'What business are we in?' and 'How are we going to make money out of it?' Strategy determines the direction in which the enterprise is going in relation to its environment in order to achieve sustainable competitive advantage. It is a declaration of intent which defines means to achieve ends, and is concerned with the long-term allocation of significant company resources. Strategy is a perspective on the way in which critical issues or success factors can be addressed. Strategic decisions aim to make a major and long-term impact on the behaviour and success of the organisation.

Features of strategy

Ultimately, strategy could be seen as a process for managing change, and as Digman (1990) puts it, the role of top management is becoming more one of changing things, 'so that the firm can achieve competitive advantage in each of its businesses', than running things.

As suggested by Hamel and Prahalad (1989), strategic decisions may involve trimming ambitions to match available resources but, more positively, they can mean leveraging resources to reach seemingly unattainable goals. The strategic intent of an organisation may imply a sizeable stretch, and effective managements do not ask, 'How will next year be different?' but 'What must we do differently to get closer to our strategic intent?' The role of top management is to challenge the organisation to close the gap by 'systematically building new advantages'.

The key concepts of strategy and strategic management are:

- competitive advantage
- distinctive competence
- critical success factors
- focus
- synergy
- resource allocation

Competitive advantage

The concept of competitive advantage was formulated by Michael Porter (1985). Competitive advantage, Porter asserts, arises out of a firm creating value for its customers. To achieve it, firms select markets in which they can excel and present a moving target to their competitors by continually improving their position.

To achieve competitive advantage, Porter emphasises the importance of:

- **differentiation**, which consists in offering a product or service 'that is perceived industry-wise as being unique'
- **focus** – seeing a particular buyer group or product market 'more effectively or efficiently than competitors who compete more broadly'

He then developed the concept of three generic strategies which organisations can use to gain competitive advantage. These are:

- **innovation** – being the unique producer
- **quality** – delivering high-quality goods and services to customers
- **cost leadership** – the planned result of policies aimed at 'managing away expense'

Distinctive competence

A distinctive competence can be described as an important feature which in Quinn's (1980) phrase 'confers superiority on the organization'. Distinctive competences, sometimes known as core competences, are what the organization is best at and what its special or unique capabilities are. They are what the company does especially well in comparison with its competitors. Key competences could exist in such areas as technology, innovation, marketing, delivering quality, and making good use of human and financial resources. If a company is aware of what its distinctive competences are it can concentrate on using and developing them without diverting effort into less rewarding activities.

Critical success factors

Critical success factors indicate those areas of corporate performance which are vital for the accomplishment of the organisation's mission – the things which must be done to gain competitive advantage. They have been defined by Thompson and Strickland (1990) as 'the specific outcomes crucial to success in the market place, and the functional skills with the most bearing on company profitability'.

The concept of critical success factors is similar to Porter's (1985) 'value activities', which are the means by which firms create value for their products and which are identified by his technique of 'value chain analysis'. This corresponds to Tregoe and Zimmerman's (1980) concept of the 'driving force' which consists of the company's future product-market's scope and defines the main strategic choices that must be made, namely:

- the key capabilities required to support the driving force
- size/growth guidelines
- business unit mission statements to guide resource allocation

Focus

Focus involves concentrating on the key strategic issues. As Porter (1985) defines it, in product-market terms focus is directed precisely at serving a particular product group, a segment of the product line, or a geographical market. Focus also means concentrating on those critical success factors or 'drivers' which are most likely to contribute to the attainment of goals.

Synergy

Synergy is what happens when the combined performance of a company's resources is greater than the sum of its parts. Strategic decisions seek to achieve synergy in order to maximise the joint impact of its resources.

Resource allocation

As Hofer and Schendel (1986) conclude:

> A critical aspect of top management's work today involves matching organizational competences (internal resources and skills) with the opportunities and risks created by environmental change in ways that will be both effective and efficient over the time such resources will be deployed.

Fundamentally, therefore, strategic decisions are about allocating resources to opportunities and achieving strategic fit between them.

The concept of strategy sometimes seems to be concerned exclusively with the allocation of financial resources, and the technique of portfolio planning has become fashionable. Portfolio planning is a discriminatory device for allocating resources among businesses. Its most famous manifestation is the matrix developed by the Boston Consulting Group which provides for the classification of strategic business units (SBUs) as 'stars', 'wildcats', 'cash cows' or 'dogs'. This can lead to prescriptions to withdraw from dogs, milk cash cows, develop wildcats or maintain the growth and market share of stars.

But on the basis of extensive research into portfolio planning in US companies, Hamermesh (1986) came to the conclusion that it has led to under-investment in, and the abandonment of, mature businesses; it has not helped competitiveness and could have contributed to the decline of some industries. Portfolio planning has 'inclined senior managers to concentrate on the acquisition and disposal of businesses, instead of the development of competitive strategies for them'. John Purcell (1989) has also commented that firms excessively committed to portfolio planning tend to ignore or find difficulty with that aspect of corporate strategy which determines, as Andrews (1987) put it 'the kind of economic and human organization it is or intends to be, and the nature of the economic and non-economic contribution it intends to make to its shareholders, employees, customers and communities'.

In its crudest form, a business, or indeed any type of organisation, could be regarded as a 'resource-conversion' operation where the resources consist of money, people, information or knowledge, and materials. So to what extent have the writers on business strategy referred to human resources? The answer is not much, although Andrews (1987) does suggest that the strategic role of the chief executive is to develop 'an organization capable of producing both technical achievement and human satisfaction'. Tregoe and Zimmerman (1980) state that human resource capabilities constitute one of the most critical issues in organisations and Porter (1985) asserted that 'HRM is an integral part of the value chain at firm level'.

Levels of strategy

There are four levels of business strategy:

1. **enterprise strategy**, which determines the relationships the firm has with its 'stakeholders' – that is, those such as investors, managers, employees, trade unions and the community at large which have a stake (or interest) in what the organisation does and how it does it. This enterprise strategy, as Digman (1990) puts it 'acts as a framework or envelope within which other, more specific, types of strategy will operate'.

2. **corporate strategy**, which in multi-divisional companies mainly addresses questions relating to the businesses the company should be in. It will be concerned with diversifications,

new ventures, acquisitions and divestments, and the appropriate allocation of resources among them.

3. **business-unit strategy** (which is the same for single-business companies and divisions of multi-business companies), which addresses how to compete in product-market terms. It is particularly concerned with the achievement of competitive advantage by making the best use of the firm's distinctive competences and integrating the various functional areas of the business.

4. **functional and operational strategies** in such areas as marketing, product development, manufacturing, customer service, and human resource management, which exist to support the higher-level strategies. But the enterprise and corporate strategies will not succeed unless effective support is provided in each functional area, and this is why the integrative function of business strategy is so crucial. Functional strategies are in a sense 'downstream' from enterprise and business-unit strategies which will be defined by stakeholder requirements and product-market opportunities. However, the different levels of strategy are entirely interdependent and, although the strategic thrust of an organisation will emanate from the top, the development of business and functional strategies will, or at least should, be an iterative process.

In the public and non-profit sectors it is often more appropriate to talk about 'corporate' rather than 'business' strategies, and corporate strategies in this context address the longer-term issues facing the organisation and define its intentions as to how these issues will be dealt with.

The formulation of strategy

The formulation of corporate strategy can be defined as a process for developing a sense of direction. It has often been described as a logical, step-by-step affair, the outcome of which is a formal written statement which provides a definitive guide to the organisation's long-term intentions. Many people still believe and act as if this were the case, but it is a misrepresentation of reality. This is not to dismiss completely the ideal of adopting a systematic approach as described below; it has its uses as a means of providing an analytical framework for strategic decision-making and a reference point for monitoring the implementation of strategy. But in practice, and for reasons also explained below, the formulation of strategy can never be as rational and linear a process as some writers describe it or as some managers attempt to make it.

The systematic approach to formulating strategy

In theory, the process of formulating strategy consists of the following steps:

1. Define the mission.
2. Set objectives.
3. Conduct an internal and external environmental analysis to assess internal strengths and weaknesses and external opportunities and threats (a SWOT analysis).
4. Analyse existing strategies to determine their relevance in the light of the internal and external appraisal. This may include gap analysis, which will establish the extent to which environmental factors might lead to gaps between what could be achieved if no changes were made and what needs to be achieved. The analysis would also cover resource capability, answering the question: 'Have we sufficient financial or human resources available now or which can readily be made available in the future to enable us to achieve our objectives?'
5. Define in the light of this analysis the critical success factors and distinctive competences of the organisation.
6. Define the key strategic issues emerging from the previous analysis. These will be concerned with such matters as product-market scope and resource capability.
7. Determine corporate and functional strategies for achieving goals and competitive advantage, taking into account the key strategic issues. These may include corporate strategies for

growth or diversification, or broad generic strategies for innovation, quality or cost leadership; or they may take the form of
specific corporate/functional strategies concerned with product-
market scope, technological development or human resource
development.
8. Prepare integrated strategic plans for implementing strategies.
9. Implement the strategies.
10. Monitor implementation and revise existing strategies or develop
new strategies as necessary.

This model of the process of strategy formulation should allow
scope for iteration and feedback, and the activities incorporated in
the model are all appropriate in any process of strategy formulation. But the model is essentially linear and deterministic – each
step logically follows the earlier one and is conditioned entirely by
the preceding sequence of events; and this is not what happens in
real life.

The reality of strategy formulation

It has been said (Bower, 1982) that 'strategy is everything not well
defined or understood'. This may be going too far, but in reality,
strategy formulation can best be described as 'problem solving in
unstructured situations' (Digman, 1990) and strategies will always
be formed under conditions of partial ignorance.

The difficulty is that strategies are often based on the question-
able assumption that the future will resemble the past. Some years
ago, Robert Heller (1972) attacked the cult of long-range planning:
'What goes wrong' he wrote, 'is that sensible anticipation gets con-
verted into foolish numbers: and their validity always hinges on
large loose assumptions.'

More recently, Faulkner and Johnson (1992) have said of long-
term planning that it:

> was inclined to take a definitive view of the future, and to
> extrapolate trend lines for the key business variables in order
> to arrive at this view. Economic turbulence was insufficiently
> considered, and the reality that much strategy is formulated

and implemented in the act of managing the enterprise was ignored. Precise forecasts ending with derived financials were constructed, the only weakness of which was that the future almost invariably turned out differently.

Strategy formulation is not necessarily a rational and continuous process, as has been pointed out by Mintzberg (1987). He believes that, rather than being consciously and systematically developed, strategy reorientation happens in what he calls brief 'quantum loops'. A strategy, according to Mintzberg, can be deliberate – it can realise the intentions of senior management, for example to attack and conquer a new market. But this is not always the case. In theory, he says, strategy is a systematic process: first we think, then we act; we formulate then we implement. But we also 'act in order to think'. In practice 'a realized strategy can emerge in response to an evolving situation' and the strategic planner is often 'a pattern organizer, a learner if you like, who manages a process in which strategies and visions can emerge as well as be deliberately conceived'.

Mintzberg is even more scathing in his 1994 article in the *Harvard Business Review* on 'The rise and fall of strategic planning'. He contends that 'the failure of systematic planning is the failure of systems to do better than, or nearly as well as, human beings'. He goes on to say: 'Far from providing strategies, planning could not proceed without their prior existence . . . Real strategists get their hands dirty digging for ideas, and real strategies are built from the nuggets they discover.' And 'sometimes strategies must be left as broad visions, not precisely articulated, to adapt to a changing environment'.

Other well-known writers have joined in this chorus of disapproval; for example:

> Business strategy, far from being a straightforward, rational phenomenon, is in fact interpreted by managers according to their own frame of reference, their particular motivations and information. (Pettigrew and Whipp, 1991)

> Although excellent for some purposes the formal planning approach emphasises 'measurable quantitative forces' at the

> expense of the 'qualitative, organizational and power-behav-
> ioural factors that so often determine strategic success' . . .
> Large organizations typically construct their strategies with
> processes which are 'fragmented, evolutionary, and largely
> intuitive'. (Quinn, 1980)

> The most effective decision-makers are usually creative, intu-
> itive people 'employing an adaptive, flexible process'. More-
> over, since most strategic decisions are event-driven rather
> than pre-programmed, they are unplanned. (Digman, 1990)

Goold and Campbell (1986) also emphasise the variety and ambi-
guity of influences which shape strategy:

> Informed understandings work alongside more formal processes
> and analyses. The headquarters agenda becomes entwined
> with the business unit agenda, and both are interpreted in the
> light of personal interests. The sequence of events from deci-
> sion to action can often be reversed, so that 'decisions' get
> made retrospectively to justify actions that have already taken
> place.

There is an emerging post-modernist view about change which
attacks the traditional 'modernist' concept of strategic planning
even more vigorously. Post-modernism, as defined by Kirkbride et
al. (1994), rejects reason and rationality; rejects the search for universal laws and truths; and rejects the concepts of progress and
development. The advantage of adopting a post-modernist stance
is, as Eagleton (1983) notes, 'that it allows you to drive a coach and
horses through anybody else's beliefs while not saddling you with
the inconvenience of having to adopt any yourself'.

However, the central assumption of the post-modernists that environments are neither placid or turbulent, but are really chaotic, is
noteworthy. A key feature of chaos theory is the concept of instability
and unpredictability, which means that the future is unknown.
Chaos theory, as explained by Stacey (1993), states that disorder
and randomness exist in the behaviour of systems at the specific
level, but that there is a qualitative pattern at a general, overall
level: 'The future behaves unpredictably but it always does so
according to recognizable family-like resemblances.' Kirkbride et al.

(1994) suggest that the contribution of post-modernist ideas about chaos is to challenge our traditional assumptions about change processes. Thus, they say:

- We should not assume that there is any end point to any organizational change process.
- We should realize that it may be impossible to know any more than the initial direction of change.
- We should realize that attempts to precisely define either the direction or destination of change via the use of sophisticated and quantitative planning techniques are, at best, irrelevant, and at worst, counterproductive.
- We should not assume that there is an existing and definable tool kit of change mechanisms which will work, even if we use them contingently.
- We should not assume that there will be any simple, or even necessary, correspondence between our actions in change interventions and any organizational effects.
- We should not assume that it is possible, or desirable, to identify a 'recipe' or 'map' for the organizational and environmental contexts we find ourselves in.

But while these points should be borne in mind when contemplating the development of strategies for managing change, they do not mean that it is necessary entirely to follow the teaching of Jalai-Uddin Rumi and 'sell your cleverness and buy bewilderment'. What Kirkbride et al. describe as the sophisticated modernist approach of writers like Mintzberg (1978, 1987, 1988, 1994) still has much to offer. He perceives strategy as a 'pattern in a stream of activities' and highlights the importance of the interactive process between key players. He has emphasised the concept of 'emergent strategies', and a core aspect of this process is the production of something which is new to the organisation even if this is not developed as logically as the traditional corporate planners believed to be appropriate.

Strategic management

Strategic management can be regarded as a continuing process consisting of a sequence of activities: strategy formulation, strategic planning, implementation, review, and updating. It has been defined as follows:

> Strategic management is the set of decisions and actions resulting in the formulation and implementation of strategies designed to achieve the objectives of an organization. (Pearce and Robinson, 1988)

> Strategic management is concerned with policy decisions affecting the entire organization; the overall objective being to position the organization to deal effectively with its environment. (Gunnigle and Moore, 1994)

Strategic management means that managers are looking ahead at what they need to achieve in the middle or relatively distant future. Although, as Fombrun et al. (1984) put it, they are aware of the fact that businesses, like managers, must perform well in the present to succeed in the future, they are concerned with the broader issues they are facing and the general directions in which they must go to deal with these issues and achieve longer-term objectives. They do not take a narrow or restricted view.

Strategic management deals with both ends and means. As an end it describes a vision of what something will look like in a few years' time. As a means, it shows how it is expected that the vision will be realised. Strategic management is therefore visionary management, concerned with creating and conceptualising ideas of where the organisation should be going. But it is also empirical management which decides how in practice it is going to get there.

The focus is on identifying the organisation's mission and strategies, but attention is also given to the resource base required to make it succeed. It is always necessary to remember that strategy is the means to create value. Managers who think strategically will have a broad and long-term view of where they are going. But they will also be aware that they are responsible first for planning how to allocate resources to opportunities which contribute to the implementation of strategy, and secondly, for managing these opportunities in ways which will significantly add value to the results achieved by the firm.

The purpose of strategic management has been expressed by

Rosabeth Moss Kanter (1984), who believes that strategic plans 'elicit the present actions for the future' and become 'action vehicles – integrating and institutionalizing mechanisms for change'. She goes on to say:

> Strong leaders articulate direction and save the organization from change by drift . . . They see a vision of the future that allows them to see more clearly what steps to take, building on present capacities and strengths.

But beyond this rhetoric lies the reality of managers attempting to behave strategically in conditions of uncertainty, change and turbulence, even chaos. The strategic management approach is as difficult as it is desirable, and this will have to be borne in mind when considering the concept of strategic HRM in Chapter 3.

2

▚ The Concept of HRM

The concept of HRM is often defined as a strategic approach to the management of an organisation's most valued assets – the people working there who individually and collectively contribute to the achievement of its objectives for sustainable competitive advantage. HRM can be regarded as a 'set of interrelated policies with an ideological and philosophical underpinning' (Storey, 1989).

The emphasis is on:

- the interests of management
- adopting a strategic approach
- obtaining added value from people by the processes of human resource development and performance management
- gaining commitment to the objectives and values of the organisation
- the need for a strong corporate culture
- coherence in HR policies and practices

HRM is essentially a business-orientated philosophy concerning the management of people in order to obtain added value from them and thus achieve competitive advantage. It is a philosophy that appeals to managements which are striving to beat off increasing international competition and appreciate that to do this they must invest in human resources as well as new technology.

The development of the HRM concept

The impression is sometimes gained when reading accounts of HRM that it appeared out of the blue as the result of the work of a group of Harvard professors in the mid-1980s (Beer et al., 1984), rather like Venus springing out of the ocean.

But HRM has a much longer history than that. Although the Harvard school and other American writers, especially Fombrun et al. (1984), were largely responsible for packaging it as a concept, the roots of HRM go right back to the 1930s; and through the work of a number of American and British researchers and writers, as described below, these roots have been spreading steadily ever since.

The human relations school

Elton Mayo (1933) and his colleagues emphasised people's social needs. The need for belonging was seen as providing the basic motivation for individuals to work. They believed that the social controls set up by cohesive work groups can be a powerful counter-vailing force to management's efforts to use financial rewards and organisational controls to achieve what it wants. This concept rapidly developed into the human relations school, which believed that productivity was directly related to job satisfaction and that individuals' output will be high if they like their co-workers and are given pleasant supervision.

To a certain extent, this approach was akin to paternalism, where it is assumed that people can be induced to work out of a feeling of gratitude for the system. It is therefore a precursor of the focus on commitment in the HRM philosophy – an approach which can be described as the achievement of compliance through commitment.

Another pioneer of the 1930s was Chester Barnard (1938) who wrote that 'the task of leadership is essentially one of shaping values' and thus led the way to the culture management aspect of HRM.

Peter Drucker

Peter Drucker (1955) virtually invented management by objectives (although he never actually used that phrase). He wrote: 'An effective management must direct the vision and effort of all managers towards a common goal.' This concept of visionary goal-directed leadership is fundamental to HRM.

He also castigated personnel managers for their obsession with

techniques that become gimmicks, and for their inability to get
really involved in the business. He referred to personnel management as 'a collection of individual techniques without much
internal cohesion – a hodge podge'. The emphasis in the HRM
approach on coherence and internal consistency in order to over-
come this tendency follows the Drucker line. Finally, he stressed
that human resources should be regarded as an organisational asset,
thus expressing what later became one of the basic tenets of HRM.

Douglas McGregor

McGregor (1960) advocated management by integration and self-
control as a strategy for managing people which affects the whole
business. A key role of the personnel function, as he saw it, was to
'devise means of getting management to examine its assumptions,
to consider the consequences and to compare it with others'.

   Like Drucker, McGregor therefore paved the way to the basic
HRM concept that human resource plans must be integrated with
those of the business.

The behavioural science movement

The behavioural science movement came into prominence in the
1950s and 1960s. Its leading members were:

- **Maslow** (1954), whose hierarchy of human needs placed self-
  actualisation at the top of the pyramid
- **Likert** (1966), who developed his integrating principle of supporting relationships. This stated that organisation members
  should, in the light of their values and expectations, view their
  work as supportive and as contributing to the building and maintenance of their sense of personal worth and importance
- **Argyris** (1957), who believed that organisation design should
  plan for integration and involvement and that individuals should
  feel that they have a high degree of control over setting their own
  goals and over the paths defining those goals (ie empowerment –

the discovery of the 1990s – although it was not called that in 1957)

- **Herzberg** (1957), who advocated job enrichment as a means of improving organisational effectiveness (more empowerment)

The behavioural science movement had a somewhat idealistic flavour about it, but it did make two significant contributions to the concept of HRM. First, it underlined the importance of integration and involvement, and second, it highlighted the idea that management should accept as a basic value the need to increase the quality of working life as a means of obtaining better motivation and improved results.

The organisation development movement

The organisation development (OD) movement of the 1960s and 1970s was closely associated with the concepts of the behavioural scientists. The OD approach concentrated on overall organisational effectiveness especially with regard to 'process' – how people behave in situations where they are constantly interacting with one another. Team development and the management of change were often important features of an OD programme. Particular attention was paid to the analysis of group processes, and OD consultants evolved methods of analysing organisational behaviour, especially within and between groups, and of solving conflict problems.

These concepts and approaches, especially those concerning the importance of process, were linked to the views of the excellence school and have been incorporated in both the philosophy and the methodology of HRM.

The excellence school

The excellence school consists of writers such as Pascale and Athos (1981) and Peters and Waterman (1982), who produced lists of the attributes which they claimed characterised successful companies. These popular writers have strongly influenced management thinking about the need for strong cultures and commitment.

Pascale and Athos emphasised the importance of 'superordinate goals' – the significant meanings of the guiding concepts (ie values) with which an organisation imbues its members.

Peters and Waterman suggested that the following attributes characterise the 'excellent companies':

- **Productivity through people.** The 'excellent companies' believe that the basis for productivity and quality is the workforce. They do not pay lip service to the slogan 'people are our most important asset'. Instead, they do something about it by encouraging commitment and getting everyone involved.
- **Hands-on, value-driven.** The people who run the organisation get close to those who work for them and ensure that the organisation's values are understood and acted upon.
- **Visionary leadership.** The value-shaping leader is concerned with 'soaring lofting, visions that will generate excitement and enthusiasm. Clarifying the value system and breathing life into it are the greatest contributions a leader can make.'

Peters (1988) also advocated the following approach to managing people:

> Trust people and treat them as adults, enthuse them by lively and imaginative leadership, develop and demonstrate an obsession for quality, make them feel they own the business, and you will find they will respond with total commitment.

It is worth noting, however, that some of the 'excellent' companies cited by Peters and Waterman did not maintain their success and Tom Peters, indulging in apostasy, started his book *Thriving on Chaos* (1988) with the words: 'There are no excellent companies.'

However, for managers the gospel according to Peters and the messages from other writers such as Rosabeth Moss Kanter (1989) and Richard Pascale (1990) have become the accepted texts for what may broadly be called an HRM approach. It is safe to say that these and other popular writers (for example

Blanchard and Johnson, 1983) have exerted more influence, for good or ill, on what managers believe to be good practice (even if they don't practise it) than all the academic writers put together. Interestingly enough, however, Peters has never described what he advocates as 'HRM', which lends some support to what will be one of the recurring themes of this book – that 'you don't have to call it HRM to do it'.

The matching model of HRM

One of the first explicit statements of the HRM concept was made by Fombrun et al. (1984). They asserted that HR systems and the organisation structure should be managed in a way which is congruent with organisational strategy. This was christened the 'matching model' by Boxall (1992).

The Harvard framework

The other founding fathers of HRM were Beer et al. (1984), who developed what Boxall (1992) calls the 'Harvard framework'. This framework is based on the belief that the problems of historical personnel management can only be solved:

> . . . when general managers develop a viewpoint of how they wish to see employees involved in and developed by the enterprise, and of what HRM policies and practices may achieve those goals. Without either a central philosophy or a strategic vision – which can be provided *only* by general managers – HRM is likely to remain a set of independent activities, each guided by its own practice tradition.

Beer and his colleagues were therefore the first to underline the HRM tenet that it belongs to line managers.

They also stated:

> Human resource management involves all management decisions and action that affect the nature of the relationship between the organization and its employees – its human resources.

General managers are making strategic decisions all the time and these will have a profound impact on employees. For example, introducing new technology or deciding how the company should grow involve important HRM decisions, as do some financial decisions. None of these decisions and actions resides in the personnel function.

Two features are appropriate to HRM:

1. The general manager accepts more responsibility for ensuring the alignment of competitive strategy and personnel policies and other policies that affect people.
2. The personnel staff have the mission of setting policies that govern how personnel activities are developed and implemented in ways that make them more mutually reinforcing.

Beer et al. thought that 'today, many pressures are demanding a broader, more comprehensive and more strategic perspective with regard to the organization's human resources'. These pressures have created a need for 'a longer-term perspective in managing people and consideration of people as potential assets rather than merely a variable cost'.

Walton (1985), also of Harvard, developed the concept of mutuality:

> The new HRM model is composed of policies that promote mutuality – mutual goals, mutual influence, mutual respect, mutual rewards, mutual responsibility. The theory is that policies of mutuality will elicit commitment which in turn will yield both better economic performance and greater human development.

According to Boxall (1992) the advantages of this model are that it:

- incorporates recognition of a range of stakeholder interests
- recognises the importance of 'trade-offs', either explicitly or implicitly, between the interests of owners and those of employees as well as between various interest groups
- widens the context of HRM to include 'employee influence', the organisation of work and the associated question of supervisory style

- acknowledges a broad range of contextual influences on management's choice of strategy, suggesting a meshing of both product-market and socio-cultural logics
- emphasises strategic choice – it is not driven by situational or environmental determinism.

The Harvard model has exerted considerable influence over the theory and practice of HRM, particularly in its emphasis on the fact that HRM is the concern of management in general rather than the personnel function in particular.

David Guest

David Guest (1987, 1989a, 1989b, 1991) has taken the Harvard model and developed it further by defining four policy goals which he believes can be used as testable propositions:

- **strategic integration** – the ability of the organisation to integrate HRM issues into its strategic plans, ensure that the various aspects of HRM cohere, and provide for line managers to incorporate an HRM perspective into their decision-making
- **high commitment** – behavioural commitment to pursue agreed goals, and attitudinal commitment reflected in a strong identification with the enterprise
- **high quality** – this refers to all aspects of managerial behaviour which bear directly on the quality of goods and services provided, including the management of employees and investment in high-quality employees
- **flexibility** – functional flexibility and the existence of an adaptable organisation structure with the capacity to manage innovation

Guest believes that the driving force behind HRM is 'the pursuit of competitive advantage in the market place through provision of high-quality goods and services, through competitive pricing linked to high productivity and through the capacity swiftly to innovate and manage change in response to changes in the market place or to break throughs in research and development.'

He considers that HRM values are:

- **unitarist** to the extent that they assume no underlying and inevitable differences of interest between management and workers
- **individualistic** in that they emphasise the individual-organisation linkage in preference to operating through group and representative systems.

Guest has also asserted that HRM has been 'talked up' and its impact has been on attitudes rather than behaviour.

Karen Legge

Karen Legge (1989) considers that the common themes of typical definitions of HRM are that:

> . . . human resource policies should be integrated with strategic business planning and used to reinforce an appropriate (or change an inappropriate) organizational culture, that human resources are valuable and a source of competitive advantage, that they may be tapped most effectively by mutually consistent policies that promote commitment and which, as a consequence, foster a willingness in employees to act flexibly in the interests of the 'adaptive organization's' pursuit of excellence.

Chris Hendry and Andrew Pettigrew

Hendry and Pettigrew (1990) play down the prescriptive element of the Harvard model and extend the analytical elements. As pointed out by Boxall (1992), such an approach rightly avoids labelling HRM as a single form and advances more slowly by proceeding more analytically. It is argued by Hendry and Pettigrew that 'better descriptions of structures and strategy-making in complex organizations, and of frameworks for understanding them, are an essential underpinning for HRM'.

Hendry and Pettigrew believe that as a movement, HRM

expressed a mission, to achieve a turnaround in industry: 'HRM was thus in a real sense heavily normative from the outset: it provided a diagnosis and proposed solutions.' They also suggested: 'What HRM did at this point was to provide a label to wrap around some of the observable changes, while providing a focus for challenging deficiencies – in attitudes, scope, coherence, and direction – of existing personnel management.'

John Purcell

John Purcell (1993) thinks that 'the adoption of HRM is both a product of and a cause of a significant concentration of power in the hands of management', while the widespread use 'of the language of HRM, if not its practice, is a combination of its intuitive appeal to managers and, more importantly, a response to the turbulence of product and financial markets'.

He considers that HRM policies and practices, when applied within a firm as a break from the past, are often associated with words such as commitment, competence, empowerment, flexibility, culture, performance, assessment, reward, teamwork, involvement, cooperation, harmonisation, quality and learning. But 'the danger of descriptions of HRM as modern best-management practice is that they stereotype the past and idealize the future'.

Keith Sisson

Keith Sisson (1990) suggests that there are four main features increasingly associated with HRM:

1. There is an emphasis on the integration of personnel policies both with one another and with business planning more generally.
2. The locus of responsibility for personnel management no longer resides with (or is 'relegated to') specialist managers.
3. The focus shifts from manager–trade union relations to management–employee relations, from collectivism to individualism.

4. There is a stress on commitment and the exercise of initiative, with managers now donning the role of 'enabler', 'empowerer' and 'facilitator'.

John Storey

John Storey (1993) suggests four aspects which constitute the meaningful version of HRM:

1. a particular constellation of beliefs and assumptions
2. a strategic thrust informing decisions about people management
3. the central involvement of line managers
4. reliance upon a set of 'levers' to shape the employment relationship, which are different from those used under proceduralist and joint regulative regimes typical of classical industrial relations systems.

He has written: 'In stereotyped form it [HRM] appears capable of making good each of the main shortcomings of personnel management'. The HR function becomes recognised as a central business concern and training and development assumes a higher profile: 'Its performance and delivery are integrated into line management: the aim shifts from merely securing compliance to the more ambitious one of winning commitment.'

The concept locates HRM policy formulation firmly at the strategic level and insists that a characteristic of HRM is its internally coherent approach.

He makes a distinction (1989) between the 'hard' and 'soft' versions of HRM:

- Hard HRM emphasises the quantitative, calculative and business-strategic aspects of managing the headcount resource in as 'rational' a way as for any other economic factor.
- Soft HRM traces its roots to the human-relations school; it emphasises communication, motivation and leadership.

Characteristics of HRM

The combined contributions of the writers mentioned above and others suggest that the characteristic features of HRM as a new paradigm for managing people are:

- It is a top-management driven activity.
- The performance and delivery of HRM is a line-management responsibility.
- It emphasises the need for strategic fit – the integration of business and HR strategies.
- It stresses the importance of gaining commitment to the organisation's mission and values – it is 'commitment-orientated'.
- It involves the adoption of a comprehensive and coherent approach to the provision of mutually supporting employment policies and practices, ie the development of integrated personnel policies and practices.
- Importance is attached to strong cultures and values.
- It is performance-orientated, emphasising the need for ever higher levels of achievement to meet new challenges.
- Employee relations are unitarist rather than pluralist, individual rather than collective, high-trust rather than low-trust.
- Organising principles are organic and decentralised with flexible roles and more emphasis on teamwork – flexibility and team-building are important policy goals.
- There is strong emphasis on the delivery of quality to customers and the achievement of high levels of customer satisfaction.
- Rewards are differentiated according to performance, competence or skill.

Reservations about HRM

On the face of it, HRM has much to offer, at least to management. But strong reservations have been expressed about it by a number of academics and by one practitioner, Alan Fowler (1987), in a

typically trenchant comment in *Personnel Management*. These
reservations can be summed up as follows:

- HRM does not pass muster either as a reputable theory or as an
  alternative and better form of personnel management.
- HRM is, in David Guest's (1991) words, an 'optimistic but
  ambiguous concept', it is all hype and hope.
- Even if HRM does exist as a distinct process, which many
  doubt, it is full of contradictions, manipulative, and, according
  to the Cardiff school (Blyton and Turnbull, 1992), downright
  pernicious.

HRM as a theory

Mike Noon (1992) has commented that HRM has serious deficiencies as a theory:

> It is built with concepts and propositions, but the associated
> variables and hypotheses are not made explicit. It is too com-
> prehensive . . . If HRM is labelled a 'theory' it raises expecta-
> tions about its ability to describe and predict.

HRM is simplistic

As Alan Fowler (1987) has written:

> The HRM message to top management tends to be beguilingly
> simple. Don't bother too much about the content or techniques
> of personnel management, it says. Just manage the context.
> Get out from behind your desk, bypass the hierarchy, and go
> and talk to people. That way you will unlock an enormous
> potential for improved performance.

In this regard, there are two aspects of HRM which worry many
people. The first is the HRM rhetoric which presents it as an all-or-
nothing process which is ideal for all organisations, despite the
evidence that different business environments require different
approaches.

The second concerns industrial relations. As Fowler (1987) also stated:

> At the heart of the concept is the complete identification of employees with the aims and values of the business – employee involvement but on the company's terms. Power in the HRM system remains very firmly in the hands of the employer. Is it really possible to claim full mutuality when at the end of the day the employer can decide unilaterally to close the company or sell it to someone else?

Contradictions in HRM

Karen Legge (1989) believes that the concept of HRM contains the following internal contradictions:

- the complementarity and consistency of 'mutuality' policies designed to generate commitment, flexibility, quality etc
- problems over commitment: as Guest (1987) asked: 'commitment to what?'
- an apparent contradiction between preaching the virtues of individualism (concentration on the individual) and collectivism (teamwork etc)
- a potential tension between the development of a strong corporate culture and employees' ability to respond flexibly and adaptively

The morality of HRM

In spite of all their protestations to the contrary, the advocates of HRM could be seen to be introducing alternative and more insidious forms of 'control by compliance' when they emphasise the need for employees to be committed to do what the organisation wants them to do. As Legge (1989) pointed out:

> In its emphasis on 'strong culture', in theory HRM is able to achieve a cohesive workforce, but without the attendant dilemma of creating potentially dysfunctional solidarity. For a

> 'strong culture' is aimed at uniting employees through a shared
> set of managerially sanctioned values ('quality', 'service',
> 'innovation' etc) that assume an identification of employee and
> employer interests. Such co-optation – through cultural manage-
> ment of course – reinforces the intention that autonomy will be
> exercised 'responsibly', ie in management's interests.

In other words, say the accusers, HRM is manipulative. They
note that chief executives with a mission for HRM tend to adapt the
principle of 'what is good for General Motors is good for America'
to that of 'what is good for the business must be good for everyone
in it' – in other words, like an apple a day, HRM is good for you.
Such executives could be right, but not necessarily, and the forces
of internal persuasion and propaganda may have to be deployed to
get people to accept values with which they may not be in accord
and which in any case may be against their interests.

Some commentators, especially the Cardiff school, seem to
regard HRM as totally evil. Keenoy and Anthony (1992), for
example, make the following observations:

- 'A wide and contradictory variety of regenerative initiatives have
  been introduced under the name of HRM and force-fed to a bat-
  tered, bewildered and defensive workforce and a newly confident
  management.'
- 'The fundamental message is one designed to construct certainty in
  a context where none exists . . . Such a script echoes the timeless
  exhortations of all ideological tyrannies . . . Unlike more familiar
  total ideologies which have sought the 'real' perfect society in universal socialism, Aryan supremacy or religious salvation, HRM
  pursues a safer but more risible objective: the excellent pretzel.'
- HRM is the 'medium for the nurturing of a new reality. It is concerned with the management of beliefs, with the manufacture of
  acquiescence in corporate values, with the production of images.'
- HRM is characterised 'by obscure origins, seemingly endless
  internal contradictions, the absence of significant empirical support and a constant process of conceptual elision.' It can be
  regarded as an 'archetypal and unredeemable Jamesonian post-
  modernist cultural product'.

The practicality of HRM

To put the concept of HRM into practice would involve strategic integration, developing a coherent and consistent set of employment policies, and gaining commitment. This requires high levels of determination and competence at all levels of management and a strong and effective personnel function staffed by business-orientated people. It is difficult to meet these criteria, especially when the proposed HRM culture conflicts with traditional managerial attitudes and behaviour.

It is claimed by some opponents of the HRM concept that the development of integrated HR strategies, a central feature of HRM, is difficult if not impossible in companies which lack any real sense of strategic direction. Business strategies, they say, where they *are* formulated, tend to be dominated by product-market imperatives, leading to product and systems developments. To support these, priority is given, understandably enough, to obtaining financial resources and maintaining a sound financial base. Human resource considerations often come a poor second.

HRM and personnel management

In the words of David Guest (1989b): 'HRM and personnel management Can you tell the difference?'

An earlier answer to this question was made by Armstrong (1987):

> HRM is regarded by some personnel managers as just a set of initials or old wine in new bottles. It could indeed be no more and no less than another name for personnel management, but as usually perceived, at least it has the virtue of emphasising the virtue of treating people as a key resource, the management of which is the direct concern of top management as part of the strategic planning processes of the enterprise. Although there is nothing new in the idea, insufficient attention has been paid to it in many organisations. The new bottle or label can help to overcome that deficiency.

Derek Torrington (1989) argued:

> Personnel management has grown through assimilating a
> number of additional emphases to produce an ever-richer
> combination of expertise . . . HRM is no revolution but a fur-
> ther dimension to a multi-faceted role.

This view that 'it's all the same really' was summed up by Pat
Lowry (1990), a former President of the Institute of Personnel
Management when he pointed out:

> Personnel work has always included strategic matters and the
> present emphasis on business issues merely represents another
> change in the environment to which the personnel manager
> adapts by strengthening the competences needed for the new
> situation. Human resource management is just the continuing
> process of personnel management – it is not different.

This is a convincing argument, but it could be said that awareness
amongst personnel directors and managers of the need to be more
strategically and business-orientated might not have developed to
its present state without the influence of the HRM concept.

Similarities

It can be argued that the similarities between personnel management and HRM are as follows:

- Personnel management strategies, like HRM strategies, flow
  from the business strategy.
- Personnel management, like HRM, recognises that line managers
  are responsible for managing people. The personnel function
  provides the necessary advice and support services to enable
  managers to carry out their responsibilities.
- The values of personnel management and at least the 'soft' version of HRM are identical with regard to 'respect for the individual', balancing organisational and individual needs, and
  developing people to achieve their maximum level of competence both for their own satisfaction and to facilitate the achievement of organisational objectives.

- Both personnel management and HRM recognise that one of their most essential processes is that of matching people to ever-changing organisational requirements – placing and developing the right people in and for the right jobs.
- The same range of selection, competence analysis, performance management, training, management development and reward management techniques are used in both HRM and personnel management.
- Personnel management, like the 'soft' version of HRM, attaches importance to the processes of communication and participation within an employee-relations system.

Differences

The differences between personnel management and HRM can be seen as a matter of emphasis and approach rather than one of substance. Or, as Hendry and Pettigrew (1990) put it, HRM can be perceived as a 'perspective on personnel management and not personnel management itself'.

From her review of the literature, Legge (1989) has identified three features which seem to distinguish HRM and personnel management:

1. Personnel management is an activity aimed primarily at non-managers whereas HRM is less clearly focused but is certainly more concerned with managerial staff.
2. HRM is much more of an integrated line-management activity whereas personnel management seeks to influence line management.
3. HRM emphasises the importance of senior management being involved in the management of culture whereas personnel management has always been rather suspicious of organisation development and related unitarist, social-psychologically orientated ideas.

The strategic nature of HRM is another difference commented on by a number of people who, in effect, dismiss the idea that traditional personnel management was ever really involved in the strategic areas of business. Hendry and Pettigrew (1990), for example, believe that the strategic character of HRM is distinctive.

Perhaps the most significant difference is that the concept of HRM is based on a management- and business-orientated philosophy. It is claimed to be a central, senior-management-driven strategic activity which is developed, owned and delivered by management as a whole to promote the interests of the organisation which they serve. It purports to be a holistic approach concerned with the total interests of the organisation – the interests of the members of the organisation are recognised but subordinated to those of the enterprise. Hence the importance attached to strategic integration and strong cultures, which flow from top management's vision and leadership, and which require people who will be committed to the strategy, who will be adaptable to change, and who will fit the culture. By implication, as Guest (1991) says: 'HRM is too important to be left to personnel managers.'

Conclusions

It is probably true that there is no such thing as a universal model of HRM. It is certainly true that when comparing the concepts of HRM personnel management all that happens is the production of distinctions without differences. As David Guest (1989a) has written: 'The HRM model is just one among a variety of forms of personnel management, and for some companies it may not be the most viable.'

Perhaps HRM should be regarded simply as a notion of how people can best be managed *in the interests of the organisation*. This echoes Torrington and Hall's (1991) argument that personnel management is *workforce centred* and therefore directs itself to employees, while HRM is *resource centred* and concerns itself with the overall human resource needs of the organisation.

If this distinction is allowed, then concepts such as strategic integration, culture management, commitment and total quality management, and a unitary philosophy (the interests of management and employees coincide) fit in well with the HRM model. Certainly, these notions have entered into the vocabulary of managers and support the idea that something which could be broadly described as strategic HRM (although they may not use this phrase) will help them to improve organisational performance in the longer term.

There can be no doubt that there is something, whether you like it or not, which can be described as an HRM philosophy. But it can be put into practice by people who are described as personnel directors just as well or even better than those who have been retitled human resource directors. HRM can be seen as an approach to personnel management which is shared between line managers and personnel specialists and which, amongst other things, emphasises the strategic nature of personnel management as a process which exists to enable the organisation to achieve its objectives and, importantly, provide for the needs of its stakeholders. Strategic HRM, as discussed in the next chapter, is a convenient label to attach to this approach, and seems to have gained a measure of general acceptability as such (hence the title of this book) but it could equally well be called strategic personnel management.

3

■ The Concept of Strategic HRM

Strategic HRM defined

Strategic HRM is an approach to making decisions on the intentions of the organisation concerning people which are an essential component of the organisation's corporate or business strategy. It is about the relationship between HRM and strategic management in the organisation. Strategic HRM refers to the overall direction the organisation wishes to pursue in achieving its objectives through people. It is argued that, because in the last analysis it is people who implement the strategic plan, top management must take this key factor fully into account in developing its corporate strategies. Strategic HRM, in this perspective, is an integral part of those strategies.

Strategic HRM addresses broad organisational concerns relating to changes in structure and culture, organisational effectiveness and performance, matching resources to future requirements and the management of change. Overall, it will consider any major 'people' issues which affect or are affected by the strategic plan of the organisation.

Wright and Snell (1989) have suggested that in a business, strategic HRM deals with 'those HR activities used to support the firm's competitive strategy'. Another business-orientated definition was provided by Miller (1989) as follows:

> Strategic human resource management encompasses those decisions and actions which concern the management of employees at *all levels* in the business and which are directed towards creating and sustaining *competitive advantage*.

Walker (1992) defined strategic HRM as 'the means of aligning the management of human resources with the strategic content of the business' and Boxall (1994) expressed the view that 'the critical concerns of human resource management are integral to strategic management in any business'.

Aim of strategic HRM

Strategic HRM aims to provide a sense of direction in an often turbulent environment so that organisational and business needs can be translated into coherent and practical policies and programmes. Strategic HRM should provide guidelines for successful action and the ultimate test of the reality of strategic HRM is the extent to which it has stimulated such action.

Strategic HRM and HR strategies

The terms strategic HRM and HR strategy are often used interchangeably, but a distinction can be made between them.

Strategic HRM can be regarded as a general approach to the strategic management of human resources in accordance with the intentions of the organisation on the future direction it wants to take. By this definition, strategic HRM is integrated with the processes of strategic management adopted by the organisation. What emerges from this process is a stream of decisions over time which form the pattern adopted by the organisation for managing its human resources and define the areas in which specific HR strategies need to be developed. As described by Tyson and Witcher (1994), these strategies describe 'the intentions and plans for utilizing human resources to achieve business objectives'.

Strategic HRM can therefore be regarded as an overall approach to dealing with longer-term people issues as part of the strategic management processes of the organisation. It will deal with macro-concerns about structure, values, culture, quality, commitment, performance, competence and management development. HR strategies will focus on the specific intentions of the organisation on what needs to be done and what needs to be changed. The issues with which these strategies may be concerned include ensuring that the organisation has the people it needs, training, motivation, reward, flexibility, team working and stable employee relations. These are the issues which facilitate the successful achievement of the corporate strategy.

According to this analysis, strategic HRM decisions are built into
the strategic plan while HR strategy decisions are derived from it.
But the process of formulating such strategies should not be seen as
a passive one. The strategic HRM concept requires that their thrust
and purpose should be determined while developing the overall
strategy and this could well be an iterative process.

To sum up, it could be said that the relationship between strategic
HRM and HR strategies is comparable with the relationship between
strategic management and corporate or business strategies. Both
strategic HRM and strategic management are terms which describe
an approach which may be adopted by top management which
focuses on longer-term issues and setting the overall direction. HR
and corporate/business strategies can be outcomes of this approach
which specify in more detail the intentions of the organisation concerning key issues and particular functions or activities.

However, this distinction should not be pursued too rigorously.
The concept of strategic HRM embraces both the overall approach
and the manifestations of that approach in the form of specific HR
strategies. When assessing the reality of the concept of strategic
HRM it will be necessary to consider both these aspects.

Origins of the concept

The concept of strategic HRM was first formulated by Fombrun et
al. (1984) who wrote that three core elements are necessary for
firms to function effectively:

- mission and strategy
- organisation structure
- human resource management

They defined strategy as a process through which the basic mission
and objectives of the organisation are set, and a process through
which the organisation uses its resources to achieve its objectives.

They also made a distinction between the three levels of managerial work:

1. **strategic level** – policy formulation and overall goal setting
2. **managerial level** – concerned with the availability and allocation of resources to carry out the strategic plan
3. **operational level** – day-to-day management

But their most important conclusion was that 'HR systems and organisational structures should be managed in a way which is congruent with organisational strategy'.

The rationale for strategic HRM

The rationale for strategic HRM rests on the perceived advantage of having an agreed and understood basis for developing approaches to managing people in the longer term. The rationale also contains the belief that declarations of intent in HRM should be integrated with the needs of both the organisation and the people in it.

It has also been suggested by Lengnick-Hall and Lengnick-Hall (1990) that underlying this rationale in a business is the concept of achieving competitive advantage through HRM:

> Competitive advantage is the essence of competitive strategy.
> It encompasses those capabilities, resources, relationships and
> decisions which permit an organization to capitalize on oppor-
> tunities in the marketplace and to avoid threats to its desired
> position.

Increasingly, they claim, it is being acknowledged that the management of people is one of the key links to generating a competitive edge.

This rationale accepts the fact that the degree to which the concept of strategic HRM can be applied within organisations and its form and content will vary widely. It is recognised that organisations can be so preoccupied with survival and managing the here and now that, unwisely perhaps, they will not have an articulated corporate or business strategy. In these circumstances, which are typical of many organisations in the UK where 'short-termism' in times of recession has prevailed, strategic HRM will not happen. A strategic approach to HR issues will only take place in an environment in which there is a strategic approach to corporate or business issues. In many organisations – probably the great majority – the personnel function will be carrying out a primarily administrative and service role and will not be at all concerned with strategic matters. This is one of the realities of strategic HRM. However desirable it may be as a concept, it will not be practised in many organisations.

The meaning of strategic HRM

According to Hendry and Pettigrew (1986), strategic HRM has four meanings:

1. the use of planning
2. a coherent approach to the design and management of personnel systems based on an employment policy and manpower strategy and often underpinned by a 'philosophy'
3. matching HRM activities and policies to some explicit business strategy
4. seeing the people of the organisation as a 'strategic resource' for the achievement of 'competitive advantage'.

The main features of strategic HRM as defined by Dyer and Holder (1988) are:

- **Organisational level.** Because strategies involve decisions about key goals, major policies and the allocation of resources they tend to be formulated at the top.
- **Focus.** Strategies are business-driven and focus on organisational effectiveness; thus in this perspective people are viewed primarily

as resources to be managed toward the achievement of strategic business goals.

- **Framework.** Strategies by their very nature provide unifying frameworks which are at once broad, contingency-based and integrative. They incorporate a full complement of HR goals and activities designed specifically to fit extant environments and to be mutually reinforcing or synergistic.
- **Roles.** As the foregoing suggests, strategy-making generally is the responsibility of line managers, with personnel playing a supportive role.

Strategic integration: integrating corporate and human resource strategy

The whole concept of strategic HRM is predicated on the belief that HR strategies should be integrated with corporate or business strategies. Miller (1989) believes that for this state of affairs to exist it is necessary to ensure that management initiatives in the field of HRM are *consistent* – consistent with those decisions taken in other functional areas of the business, and consistent with an analysis of the product-market situation.

The key is to make operational the concept of 'fit' – the fit of human resource management with the strategic thrust of the organisation. The development of operational linkages is what strategic HRM is all about. Tyson and Witcher (1994) consider that 'human resource strategies can only be studied in the context of corporate and business strategies'.

Strategic integration is necessary to provide congruence between business and human resource strategy so that the latter supports the accomplishment of the former and, indeed, helps to define it. The aim is to provide strategic fit and consistency between the policy goals of HRM and the business.

This point was originally made by Fombrun et al. (1984) who said:

> Just as firms will be faced with inefficiencies when they try to implement new strategies with outmoded structures, so they will also face problems of implementation when they attempt to effect new strategies with inappropriate HR systems. The critical management task is to align the formal structure and the HR systems so that they drive the strategic objectives of the organization.

Guest (1989b) has suggested that strategic HRM is largely about integration. One of his key policy goals, as listed in Chapter 2, is to ensure that HRM 'is fully integrated into strategic planning so that HRM policies cohere both across policy areas and across hierarchies and HRM practices are used by line managers as part of their everyday work'.

Walker (1992) has pointed out that HR strategies are functional strategies like financial, marketing, production or IT strategies. In many organisations long-range functional planning is a mandated element of the long-range business-planning process.

HR strategies are different, however, in the sense that they are intertwined with all other strategies. The management of people is not a distinct function but the means by which all business strategies are implemented. HR planning should be an integral part of all other strategy formulations. Where it is separate, it needs to be closely aligned.

Problems of integration

This is easier said than done for the following reasons:

Diversity of strategic processes, levels and styles   The different levels at which strategy is formulated, as described in Chapter 1, and the different styles adopted by organisations, may make it difficult to develop a coherent view of what sort of HR strategies will fit the overall strategies and what type of HR contributions are required during the process of formulation.

It has been argued by Miller (1987) that to achieve competitive advantage, each business unit in a diversified corporation should tailor its HRM policy to its own product-market conditions, irre-spective of the HRM policies being pursued elsewhere in the cor-poration. If this is the case, there may be coherence within a unit but not across the whole organisation and it may be difficult to focus HR strategies on corporate needs. In a 'financial control' type of corporation, as defined by Goold and Campbell (1986), ie one in which the centre is mainly concerned with financial results which they control against targets, there may be no pressure for the cre-ation of a corporate culture and HR strategies to support it at the centre. But need this matter? The centre may exercise financial control while the strategic business units (SBUs) would be allowed to go their own way so far as strategic HRM is concerned, as long as they deliver the financial results expected of them. And there is no reason why the SBUs should not decide independently that the best way to achieve those results is to pursue their own version of strategic HRM.

The only time a serious problem is likely to emerge is if units have to be merged. Admittedly, synergy may have to be sacrificed and the organisation might not reap the benefits of a corporate man-agement-development and career-planning strategy. But that choice has been made by those who are in command of such organisations and if it is their loss, it is only they who can do anything about it.

The complexity of the strategy formulation process   As Hendry and Pettigrew (1986) maintain, strategy formulation and implemen-tation is a complex, interactive process heavily influenced by a variety of contextual and historical factors. In these circumstances, as David Guest (1991) has asked, how can there be a straightfor-ward flow from the business strategy to the HR strategy?

The evolutionary nature of business strategy   This phenomenon, and the incremental nature of strategy-making, may make it diffi-cult to pin down the HR issues which are likely to be relevant. Hendry and Pettigrew (1990) suggest that there are limits to the extent to which rational HR strategies can be drawn up if the process of business strategic planning is itself irrational. Even if Mintzberg's (1978) description of strategy as a pattern in a stream of decisions over time is accepted, it may be difficult to 'fit' HR strategy into the process in any well-defined way. HR strategies would therefore have to be equally evolutionary and just as difficult to pin down to a set of definitive statements. If this is the case, why bother to seek the holy grail of strategic fit, which implies a certain rigidity which is not in keeping with the realities of organisational life and the chaotic conditions in which organisations have to exist?

The absence of articulated business strategies   If, because of their evolutionary nature, the business strategy has not been clearly articulated, this would add to the problems of clarifying the business strategic issues which HR strategies should address. But it should be noted that 'articulation' in this context means that the business strategies are fully understood by those concerned. It does *not* mean that they have to be written down, although this may help to create understanding.

The qualitative nature of HR issues   Business strategies tend, or at least aim, to be expressed in the common currency of figures and hard data on portfolio management, growth, competitive position, market share, profitability etc. HR strategies may deal with quantifiable issues such as resourcing and skill acquisition but are equally likely to refer to qualitative factors such as commitment, motivation, good employee relations and high employment standards. The relationship between the pursuit of policies in these areas and individual and organisational performance may be difficult to establish.

Integration with what?   The concept of strategic HRM implies that HR strategies must be totally integrated with corporate/business strategies in the sense that they both flow from and contribute to such strategies. But as Brewster (1993) argues, HR strategy will be subjected to considerable environmental pressure, for example, in Europe, legislation about involvement. These may mean that HR strategies cannot be entirely governed by the corporate/business strategy.

The question also needs to be asked: 'To what extent should HR strategy take into account the interests of all the stakeholders in the organisation, employees in general as well as owners and management?'

In Storey's (1989) terms 'soft strategic HRM' will place greater emphasis on the human relations aspect of personnel management, stressing security of employment, continuous development, communication, involvement and the quality of working life. 'Hard strategic HRM' on the other hand will emphasise the yield to be obtained by investing in human resources in the interests of the business. As Lengnick-Hall and Lengnick-Hall (1990) put it:

> There is now a growing realization that the overriding concern should be the yield from employees. Yield concentrates on the intricate web of costs and benefits that result from investing in and focusing human resource activities toward a certain set of activities and away from other behaviours and attitudes. Yield recognises both trade-offs and choices. Yield depends on shared responsibilities and collaboration across functional units and hierarchical levels.

Ideally, strategic integration should attempt to achieve a proper balance between the hard and soft elements. The emphasis may be on achieving corporate or business objectives but this should be a process of planning with people in mind, taking into account the needs and aspirations of all the members of the organisation.

The concept of strategic fit

The concept of 'strategic fit' may be beguiling, but it is a difficult one. David Guest (1991) wondered whether the fit should be to business strategy, a set of values about the quality of working life or the stock of human resources, or what? He also asked:

- Are there inevitable conflicts between the different types of fit?
- How do we identify or measure fit?
- How do we integrate the various HRM policies?

Neither he nor anyone else has been able to supply definitive

answers to these questions although Walker (1992) has put forward a useful analytical model for assessing the degree of fit or
integration. He suggests that the following three types of
processes are used in developing and implementing HR strategy:

1. **The integrated process.** In this approach, HR strategy is an
   integral part of the business strategy, along with all the other
   functional strategies. In strategy review discussions, HR issues
   are addressed as well as financial, product-market and operational ones. However, the focus is not on 'downstream' matters
   such as staffing, individual performance or development but
   rather on people-related business issues, resource allocation, the
   implications of internal and external change and the associated
   goals, strategies and action plans.
2. **The aligned process.** In this approach, HR strategy is developed together with the business strategy. They may be presented
   and discussed together but they are distinct outcomes of parallel
   processes. By developing and considering them together 'there
   is some likelihood that they will influence each other and be
   adopted as a cohesive or at least an adhesive whole'.
3. **The separate process.** In this, the most common approach, a distinct HR plan is developed. It is both prepared and considered
   separately from the overall business plan. It may be formulated
   concurrently with strategic planning, before it (and an input to), or
   following it (to examine its implications). The environmental
   assessment is wholly independent. It focuses on HR issues and, so
   far as possible, looks for the 'business-relativeness' of the information obtained. Since the assessment is outside the strategic
   planning process, consideration of business strategy depends on a
   review of the current and past business strategies. The value of the
   HR strategy is therefore governed by the sufficiency (or insuffi-
   ciency) of the business-related data. This approach perpetuates the
   notion of HR as a staff-driven, functionally specialist concern.

The concept of coherence

Another aspect of strategic HRM is the concept of coherence. This could be described as the development of a mutually reinforcing set of personnel and employment policies and programmes which jointly contribute to the achievement of the organisation's strategies for matching resources to organisational needs, improving performance and quality and, in commercial enterprises, achieving competitive advantage.

In one sense, strategic HRM is holistic; it is concerned with the organisation as a total entity and addresses what needs to be done across the organisation as a whole in order to enable it to achieve its corporate strategic objectives. It is not interested in isolated programmes and techniques, or in the *ad hoc* development of personnel policies and programmes.

In their discussion of the four policy areas of HRM (employee influence, HRM flow, reward systems and work systems) Beer et al. (1984) suggested that this framework can stimulate managers to plan how to accomplish the major HRM tasks 'in a unified, coherent manner rather than in a disjointed approach based on some combination of past practice, accident and *ad hoc* response to outside pressures'.

David Guest (1989b) includes in his set of propositions about HRM as listed in Chapter 2 (pages 25 to 26) the point that strategic integration is about, *inter alia*, the ability of the organisation to ensure that the various aspects of HRM cohere. But how this ideal of coherence is achieved remains somewhat elusive. John Storey (1992b) has cast some doubts on the extent to which coherence was being achieved in 15 major British companies. Most of the cases failed to show much in the way of an integrated approach to employee practices management and there was little evidence of strategic integration with the corporate plan. As Storey pointed out:

> This finding lends some support to the view that the 'HRM model' is itself not a coherent, integrated phenomenon. Many of the initiatives recorded in the case research arise for divers reasons and in practice they showed little in common.

But this research was conducted some time ago (1986–8) and the evidence from our 1994 research as set out in Chapter 5 contradicted these findings.

One way of looking at the concept is to say that some measure of coherence will be achieved if there is an overriding strategic imperative or driving force such as quality, performance or the need to develop skills and competences, and if this initiates various processes and policies which are designed to link together and operate in concert to deliver certain defined results. For example, if the driving force were to improve performance, competence profiling techniques could be used to specify recruitment standards, identify learning and development needs and indicate the standards of behaviour or performance required. The competence frameworks could be used as the basis for human resource planning, in development centres. They could also be incorporated into a performance management system in which the aims are primarily developmental and competences are used as criteria for reviewing behaviour and assessing learning and development needs. Job evaluation could be based on levels of competence, and competence-based pay systems could be introduced. This ideal will be difficult to achieve as a 'grand design' which can be put into immediate effect, and may have to be developed progressively. Thus any snapshot research is likely to reveal gaps and inconsequentialities in personnel policies and practices. And this is what was revealed in a number of the organisations we studied, as described in Chapter 5. But in many of them, there was a clear understanding of the direction they wanted to go in achieving coherence and the steps they wanted to take to get there. Two of the directors we interviewed likened this process to assembling a jigsaw puzzle: the overall picture is known, and progressively the interlocking pieces are fitted together to complete it. Some are easier to fit in than others and the picture may take a long time to finish. This simile, however, fails to explain that what is presented to most strategists is a moving picture, not the static scene represented in a jigsaw. But it does illustrate the fact that the process of developing coherent personnel policies is likely to be an incremental one. While the piecemeal approach decried by commentators such as Guest (1989b) may not conform to an ideal model of what strategic HRM should look like, it is in practice what most organisations have to do unless they are opening on a greenfield site or going through a complete programme of regeneration.

Formulation of HR strategy

It is necessary to underline the interactive (not unilinear) relationship between business strategy and HRM, as Hendry and Pettigrew
(1990) have done. They emphasise the limits of excessively ration-*f*
alistic models of strategic and HR planning. It is also necessary to
stress that coherent and integrated HR strategies are only likely to
be developed if the top team understands and acts upon the
strategic imperatives associated with the employment, development
and motivation of people, and this will be achieved more effectively if there is a personnel director who is playing an active and
respected role as a business partner.

Many different approaches may be adopted to the formulation of
HR strategies, as our research confirmed – there is no one right
way. A similar point was also made by Tyson and Witcher (1994)
on the basis of their research in 30 well-known companies:

The different approaches to strategy formation reflect different
ways to manage change and different ways to bring the people part
of the business into line with business goals.

In strategic HRM, process may be as important as content. Tyson
and Witcher (1994) also noted from their research that:

> The process of formulating HR strategy was often as impor-
> tant as the content of the strategy ultimately agreed. It was
> argued that by working through strategic issues and high-
> lighting points of tension, new ideas emerged and a consensus
> over goals was found.

A distinction is made by Purcell (1989) between three kinds of
decision:

1. **'Upstream' first-order decisions** are concerned with the long-
   term direction of the enterprise or the scope of its activities.
2. **'Downstream' second-order decisions** are concerned with
   internal operating procedures and how the firm is organised to
   achieve its goals – compare Chandler's (1962) dictum that
   structure follows strategy.
3. **'Downstream' third-order decisions** are concerned with choices

on HR structures and approaches and are strategic in the sense that they establish the basic parameters of employee relations management in the firm.

It can indeed be argued that HR strategies, like all other functional strategies such as marketing, manufacturing and the introduction of new technology, will be developed within the context of the overall enterprise or corporate strategy, but this need not imply that HR strategies come third in the pecking order. Certainly our observations in the 10 organisations we visited were that there were only two levels of strategy formulation:

1. the corporate strategy relating to the vision, mission and objectives of the organisation and the business it is in or aspires to be in
2. the specific strategies within the corporate strategy concerning product-market development, acquisitions and divestments, human resources, finance, new technology, organisation and such overall aspects of management as quality, flexibility, productivity, innovation and cost reduction

There was no question of HR considerations being relegated to some sort of third division.

Boxall (1993) has drawn up the following propositions about the formulation of HR strategy from the literature:

- There is typically no single HR strategy in a firm (although our research showed that a number of the firms we contacted *did* have an overall strategic approach within which there were specific HR strategies).
- Business strategy may be an important influence on HR strategy but it is only one of several factors and the relationship is not unilinear.
- Implicit (if not explicit) in the mix of factors that influence the shape of HR strategies is a set of historical compromises and trade-offs from stakeholders.
- Management may seek to shift the historical pattern of HR

strategy significantly in response to major contextual change, but not all managements will respond in the same way or equally effectively.

- The strategy formation process is complex, and excessively rationalistic models that advocate formalistic linkages between strategic planning and HR planning are not particularly helpful to our understanding of it.
- Descriptions of the dimensions that underpin HR strategies are critical to the development of useful typologies but remain controversial, as no one set of constructs has established an intellectual superiority over the others.

The approaches adopted by the organisations covered by our research are described in the next chapter and the general considerations affecting the development of HR strategies are discussed in Chapter 10.

Conclusions

The fundamental concept of strategic HRM is based on the assumption that human resource strategy can contribute to the business strategy but is also justified by it. The validity of this concept depends on the extent to which it is believed that people create added value and should therefore be treated as a strategic resource. If this assumption is accepted, and it is somewhat difficult to challenge, then the validity of the concept of strategic HRM does depend on the extent to which it can be applied in practice and the outcomes of such applications. The rest of this book will explore these issues.

In Part Two the reality of strategic HRM in the 10 organisations we studied will be tested against the following 10 criteria:

1. Can the top management of the organisation be described as adopting a strategic management approach?
2. Is there a process for developing corporate/business strategies?

3. Do these strategies clearly express the intentions of top management?

4. Can the top management of the organisation be described as adopting a strategic HRM approach (although they may not use that term)?

5. Does this approach result in the development of HR strategies which address the key longer-term people issues of the organisation, clearly express the intentions of top management and are acted upon?

6. Have the HR strategies been integrated with the corporate/business strategies? To what extent can they be described in Walker's (1992) terms as 'integrated', 'aligned' or 'separate'?

7. Is there at least some degree of coherence in the personnel policies and programmes developed as a result of these strategies?

8. To what extent do the approaches adopted conform to the meanings of strategic HRM as defined by Hendry and Pettigrew (1986) as set out earlier in this chapter (page 42)?

9. To what extent can the organisation be described as pursuing the four policy goals defined by Guest (1989) as set out in Chapter 2 (page 25)?

10. Have the strategies provided effective guidelines for decision-making and have they been acted on?

Part Three will explore in more detail aspects of implementing, managing and evaluating strategic HRM and approaches to formulating HR strategies.

Part Two:

Strategic HRM for Real

4

♟ Strategic HRM in Action – the formulation of strategy

The approaches adopted by the eight companies in which we saw a number of members of the top management team are summarised below, mainly in their own words, on the grounds that this is the best way of conveying the reality of their strategic management processes.

Taking into account Tyson and Witcher's (1994) point that you can only study HR strategy in the context of corporate and business strategies, we describe the processes of formulating both corporate/business strategies and HR strategies.

ABC Distribution

Background

ABC Distribution distributes food products, mainly to major retailers. The critical success factors for the organisation as spelt out by its Managing Director and the Finance Director are its ability to meet its profit targets and to grow the business substantially on a consistent basis by developing a reputation for providing added-value services, developing business with existing customers, winning new customers, and acquisitions. The company has doubled in size in the last four years. Underpinning the development of the company are the needs to grow the infrastructure, to develop management and leadership and to extend quality and safety programmes.

Business strategy

The Managing Director agreed that in a sense their business

strategy evolved in a semi-formal way, but this evolution took place
'by the key people understanding what the total business was trying
to do, and their part in it; then they went away and put their bits
together; then we pulled all of it together'. He commented: 'Our
strategy is very simple and very broad . . . It can be put down in a
few sentences. It's what lies around it that has to be developed.'
    He emphasised that:

> We sought to demonstrate to the rest of the business that we
> [the Board] were a team. Where a team hadn't existed before,
> a team was now running the company.

The Deputy Managing Director explained how he saw the formulation of the business strategy taking place:

> We put our strategy together within the framework of the
> financial targets we have to meet and our values for quality,
> integrity and management style.

In answer to the question, 'How does your organisation develop
its business strategies?', the Director of Finance said:

> It started off as being very simple in that we had an objective
> to grow in excess of the rate of growth demanded by our
> parent company . . . However, that process has become less
> naïve, more detailed and more structured as the business
> grows . . . I see planning as a process that goes on and on and
> on and becomes more complex and more refined.

He also made the following interesting comment: 'Don't forget,
not all strategies necessarily involve massive change. You can have
a strategy to stay as you are.'
    The Director of Network Business emphasised the dynamic
nature of strategy in a growing business operating in a highly competitive environment:

> We have a strategy document which is concerned with devel-
> oping market share and growth and is being continuously
> updated . . . The update is driven by the Board . . . We have to
> make sure that we continue to refresh the strategy.

The Director of Personnel commented:

> The longer-term strategy is developed basically by the Board getting together and working its way through . . . We also share that plan with the senior management team.

HR strategy

The Managing Director described their approach to developing the HR strategy as follows:

> Our HR strategy has to respond to our business needs . . . So we start with a business plan; we know we are going to grow at a certain rate. Then we do a skills audit and predict how many managers we are going to need. Our of this comes our HR development policy on skills training, leadership training and recruitment.

The Deputy Managing Director thought that the Director of Personnel was basically responsible for developing their HR strategy:

> We all look at our business strategy and express a view on the people we need, but our HR Director pulls it all together and interprets our ramblings into something coherent.

However, in answering a question on how HR strategies were developed, the Director of Finance admitted:

> We probably have more HR policies than strategies because the strategies are there in a simple sense but not 100 per cent well articulated – for valid reasons; we are a growing business.

The Director or Personnel referred to the way in which strategic initiatives were developed:

> First the personnel people meet and we bounce ideas about and seek ideas. Then if we have a new initiative we put it to the Board for discussion.

Bookworld

Background – critical success factors

Bookworld is a major and highly successful publishing company which has always been very much market-orientated. The Financial Director suggested that the overriding success factor has been that:

> We have always had very good staff at all levels. We seem always to have people who are committed, people who are prepared to give more than their contract says they should, and people who get things done . . . And the sort of informal culture we have encourages these people to stay.

The Marketing Director described the company as 'a very hands-on business' and the Financial Director commented:

> A lot of our style is about immediacy. It's about what has to be done now. That is not to say there is no planning: we have a strategic plan and budgets and forecasting; but we are more of a 'now' company in the sense that we tend mainly to think about today and what we need to do today to make tomorrow better.

The Human Resources Director said:

> The critical success factors of this organisation are the competence of the people, its willingness to change, the professionalism of its management, its forward planning, its interpersonal relationships within the company and the outside environment.

Business strategy

Commenting on the changed approach to developing the strategic plan, the Chief Executive said:

> We spent a lot of time trying to involve the whole of the senior management team. We used to present things and send people

off into syndicates to mull them over and enhance them, and then in plenary sessions we created a draft skeleton plan. We have now honed this down and restricted it to the Board because we found that managers were wandering from strategy to tactics . . .

We produce a five-year strategic plan which is distributed to senior managers. Last year we brought in outside strategic consultants who were catalytic and challenged some of the sacred cows.

When asked whether everyone on the Board was involved in this, the Chief Executive's reply was: 'They're present.'

The following comments were made by other directors on the process of formulating strategic plans:

We develop our strategies in a fairly formal way in that we have away days when we sit down as a Board and talk about strategy; and we pull out the strategic points and look ahead five years . . . We try to determine where we want to be and strategically what we need to do to be there. We do have a problem, which is probably not unique, in separating the strategic from the tactical. (Financial Director)

We produce a strategic plan which looks five years ahead which covers each area: marketing, distribution, operations and human resources. This provides an overview of the business, its strengths and weaknesses . . . The process of creating, writing and debating the strategy takes six or seven months. (Marketing Director)

The Board does go through a process of developing a corporate strategy and, process-wise, we're not bad on strategy . . . But it is not all top-down. I do get my senior managers together and ask 'What will be important to you in the future?' (Operations Director)

We have a strategic document; a strategic plan which was arrived at by general discussion and then each director has a responsibility for his part of the strategic plan; hence we have a chapter for human resourcing. (HR Director)

HR strategy

The following answers were given to the question: 'How does your organisation develop its HR strategies?'

> The HR strategy doesn't change dramatically, because it is simply that we will get the right people to meet our needs, and that we will change people and the organisation as necessary when change is needed . . . If we need a different organisation or different people, this does not fundamentally change the HR strategy. (Chief Executive)

> As Chief Executive I have to have the organisation I want, and if it doesn't marry up with any particular model that the world of HR has thrown up, well, too bad. (Chief Executive)

> I don't think we have an HR strategy. What we have is a service to assist us in getting the right people. (Marketing Director)

> I think you've constantly got to reinforce the message that that's the goal, that's where we are going and that's what we are going to do. And you've got to support people down the line but challenge them if they are not heading in the right direction. (Financial Director)

> It is very simple and two-pronged; one, the re-organisation and restructuring of the organisation and, secondly, quality people. (HR Director)

When asked what sort of contribution he got from other members of the Board towards his strategy, the HR Director's reply was: 'I get acceptance.'

Loamshire Council

Background

Loamshire Council is a district council which is generally recognised as being a very well-run and capable local authority. It is particularly good at dealing with the environment and, as the Chief Executive said: 'We tend to care so passionately about our environment that we focus an almost disproportionate amount of our resources on environmental issues'. He further commented that the critical success factors for the authority were meeting the perceived needs of the community, creating customer satisfaction with the services provided and, importantly, 'an overall appreciation of the effectiveness of members of staff and the contribution they make towards the organisation as a whole'. Another important success factor was 'the quality of relationships and the maintenance of excellent relationships within and outside the organisation'.

Corporate strategy

The following comments were made by the Chief Executive on how corporate strategy was developed:

> We do not have a single document which says 'this is the Loamshire Council corporate strategy'. What we do have are three processes which run in parallel and together represent the coporate strategy. These comprise a *general strategy* for developing services, a *management strategy* which concentrates on the managerial processes which we need to design to bring out the best in the organisation, and the *key areas* for achievement document which focuses on specific actions.

> Strategies are developed by a top-down, bottom-up process. The members of the Council, the policy-makers, debate the strategic issues from which firm strategic proposals would develop. Individual members of staff are then given opportunities to contribute . . . A distinguishing feature of all our corporate strategy work has been the opportunity for widespread involvement in the process.

> It is incredibly important that within an organisation there is somebody who has the personal responsibility for monitoring, evaluating and reviewing the effectiveness of that organisation . . . That strategic management role lies at the heart of the Chief Executive's responsibility.

The Director of Planning commented as follows on the process of strategic planning:

> The reality is you choose directions and you move in particular directions, then all sorts of things happen that you can't possibly have conceived of, and you weave these into your strategy.

> Strategy is rooted in the vision and the culture . . . Life's very complicated, there are no easy solutions, and you don't start at 'Go' when you throw a six and proceed from there. You pick up a very complex jigsaw and you work through it. But the vision helps.

On how the top team operates the Director of Planning said:

> The things we bring to the team are personal characteristics as much as the management skills we all learn at various stages. The fact that we have a spectrum of personalities strengthens the team.

HR strategy

The Chief Executive said:

> Human resource strategy has got to be owned by the top management body within an organisation. Their commitment must be absolute otherwise it simply won't be applied in practice.

> Everything flows from the corporate strategies we have set down.

> It's about having a very strong focus on the overall effectiveness of the organisation, its direction and how it's performing.

> There is commitment to, and belief in, and respect for individuals, and I think that these are very important factors in an organisation.

When asked how HR strategies were developed the Director of Personnel replied:

Initially what I did was to list all the activities in which we were currently involved in personnel and sent a questionnaire to all the directors stating 'This is what we are doing' and asking: 'Do you want us to continue doing it? If so, do you want the same, or more, or less? Are we doing it well? Could we do it better? What are the things we are not doing that you think we ought to be doing?' The next thing I did was to have two open days in which I invited managers to come in and tell us what their perceptions of personnel were. And this confirmed our eagerness to get rid of duplication and delays in personnel matters. We were fast getting in the way and holding the whole process up. And that's where we got the agreement of the organisation that empowerment should be our strategy.

On this strategy for empowerment, the Director of Technical Services remarked:

The positive aspects of the devolution of responsibility for personnel management is that it puts people management back where it should be.

Megastores

Background

Megastores is one of the country's largest and most successful high street retailers. It has a very powerful overriding commercial objective, to increase shareholder's value, and to do this by providing value-for-money products and delivering high levels of customer service.

Critical success factors

The quantifiable critical success factor is all the statistics on growth; a more intangible one is customer knowledge – the staff understanding what the company is about, employee participation. (Managing Director)

The relationship with our customers is absolutely crucial. We believe that the essence of Megastores' success hinges around two critical factors: *empathy* in understanding what they really want better than anyone else and *expertise*, in terms of developing the product or service solutions to that [need]. (Director of Central Marketing)

One key success factor for us undoubtedly has been the time and effort that we put into the training and managing of staff. (Director of Finance)

I think the end point we are all agreed on within the organisation is the increase in shareholder value and you do this by making sure that we compete well in good markets and have an operating configuration that allows us to maximise opportunities for growth. Underwriting both those critical success factors is the ability of the organisation to measure whether it is doing that; so it's about organising yourself as a company to monitor progress and to continue to evolve new strategic direction. (Director of Personnel)

Business strategy

The Managing Director made the following observations about strategic management:

Strategy is developing a route to better the business in the medium to long term.

You cannot fully maximise the business opportunities unless you've got the proper management structure to create them.

In business you have to look at the options available, make a decision and then drive that way.

In a discussion about the way in which business strategies are developed, the Managing Director explained that ideas can generate from anywhere within the organisation and are developed through the executive committee, where issues and areas for development are considered on the basis of an in-depth analysis and assessment of the market and the competitive environment.

The approach to strategy formulation was described by the Director of Finance as follows:

> Our strategy tends to be based on the resolution of issues. There is a base strategy and we continue to question whether that is the right thing to be going forward with.
>
> We have a strategic planning framework throughout the group. It's called value-based management, the fundamentals of which are to make sure that whatever you do, you must maximise shareholder value . . . It provides us with a basis for looking at what we are doing and the resources we require we've never had before.

He also commented, however:

> We're highly profitable, but in turn we invest an awful lot in our people. We spend a lot of money on the training and development of people throughout the organisation. It's probably one of our key differentiators.

The Director of Stores gave these perspectives on the strategic planning process:

> We have in place a formal business planning process in which we divide the planning into three levels. One is at business level where we identify issues that we deal with as a company, the second level is product-market planning, and the third level is local market planning.
>
> Our business strategy is formed through value-based management which is a discipline for pulling everything together and ensures that decisions are made on the basis of their real value to the business rather than someone's strength of personality or hunch. This in itself required the involvement of all the directors in a more formal business planning process. Three or four years ago we worked more individually and now we work more as a team.

Thinking about the contribution of the members of the top team to the strategy, the Director of Central Marketing observed that:

People can bring past experience and everyone brings a slightly different perspective to an issue. That perspective can be to get us as a group to think outside the 'box' within which we all operate. An individual's background perspective can sometimes bring the debate from a slightly different perspective than the company's comfort zone.

He also commented that:

There are elements of our business which are incredibly value-creating. There are others which are incredibly value-destroying. The trick is to identify the ones which are value-creating and funnel resources to them.

There are a number of blocks that make up our business strategy. The first is our overall objective. Against this we spin off a number of elements we call major initiatives. These are coordinated by our Director of Corporate Planning, but it is the functional directors who are really charged with taking ownership of these objectives. We have got a number of spin-off projects that compositely make up the business plan and will enhance the objective of maximising long-term shareholder value.

HR strategy

The following comments were made by the Managing Director and a number of other directors on the formulation of HR strategy:

The biggest challenge will be to maintain [our] competitive advantage and to do that we need to maintain and continue to attract very high-calibre people. (Managing Director)

All we do in terms of training and manpower planning is directly linked to business improvement. (Managing Director)

The key differentiator on anything any company does is fundamentally the people, and I think that people tend to forget that they are the most important asset. Money is easy to get hold of, good people are not. (Managing Director)

> The influence in terms of strategic direction must always be based on the key areas of marketing and operations. (Director of Finance)

> From a marketing standpoint the most crucial element is to look at the future needs of the customer and I think in personnel terms that is also the overriding objective. To have personnel strategies in place to recruit, develop and train the personnel resource that we have got to really satisfy these needs, I think, is really the key element – but it must be future- and customer-focused. We have to help the business achieve its objectives and the HR strategy has to be very much tailored towards those objectives. (Director of Personnel)

When questioned on his approach to the development of personnel strategies the Director of Personnel, David Roberts, replied:

> I start with the top line, the four or five things which are the strategic platform for the company. I get my managers together to look at the implications. We then pull it together so that it is all derived from the original strategic platforms and then work top-down and bottom-up to get the amalgam of what we can achieve. This then feeds into the final operating plan so we can agree budgets. ·

Morton Healthcare Trust

Background

The Morton Healthcare Trust manages one of the leading provincial teaching hospitals. As explained by the Chief Executive, the critical success factors for the Trust are:

> To deliver our contracts and this means meeting our volume and quality requirements and staying within budget . . . But if I were to say what my real management aims are, they are the preservation and development of a teaching hospital, because more important even than treating patients, is training the next generation of health carers, because if we don't do that, there will be no health service.

On the achievements of the Trust the Chief Executive commented:

> If you want to ask if we are successful, the answer is yes. We
> deliver our contracts, we're in excess by about 4 or 5 per cent
> a year, a rising target; we do so within budget and we got a
> charter mark. If you do want to measure things, the measured
> success is there, but if you ask me if I am satisfied, of course
> I'm not. We can always do better.

It is clear that the process of corporate and HR strategic planning
is quite different within the National Health Service (NHS) from
that in any of the other organisations we visited. This is partly
because of the nature of the NHS as it has developed over the last
decade. The Chief Executive's trenchant comment on its managerial approach was:

> I think people try and impose an out-of-date, industrial-style
> management structure on the Health Service which is wholly
> inappropriate. A lot of what is being attempted will fail. How
> damaging this will be is difficult to say, because one of the
> characteristics of the Health Service is that no matter how
> badly you manage it, you can't stop people treating patients. If
> the Health Service manufactured Fiestas it would have gone
> bankrupt years ago; but it doesn't, it manages management
> while the health carers get on with caring for patients, and the
> two barely interfere with one another.

Corporate strategy

On corporate strategy, the Chief Executive remarked:

> It's a misunderstanding that we can have a strategy. I don't
> believe it. We have to have a flexible response mechanism. . . .
> If we have any long-term strategy at all it is that of flexibility.

> People talk about a finance-led strategy. But you can't have a
> finance-led strategy because it's only a measurement. What
> you have to have is a commitment to provide the best possible
> care within the resources available and the people best able to

do that are at operational level; not at management level, not
at Board level and certainly not at regional level.

What was quite clear was that the approach to formulating strategy
in this organisation depended largely on the management style of
the Chief Executive and his team of directors, although this feature
applies equally well to all the other organisations we visited.

The following remarks made by the Chief Executive convey
some indication of his management style:

> I've only got two lines in my job description: if anything goes
> wrong it's my fault; if anything goes well, it's to somebody
> else's credit, because I didn't do it. I think that's the only job
> description any chief executive should have.

> I look upon myself in a sense as the cavalry behind the hill;
> and if the Indians start winning, I come along and help the
> cowboys – because it's a sort of battle all the time, isn't it, and
> I redress the balance, and nobody knows that I haven't really
> got any power at all.

> [On performance-related pay] I refuse to pay the workforce
> 97.5 per cent for failing and 2.5 per cent for succeeding. It's
> an insult, and all it does is demotivate people. I pay them 100
> per cent for succeeding and it's my job to make sure they suc-
> ceed. It's not my job to dock their pay if they don't. So we
> have a success-orientated strategy in which we expect people
> to succeed and if they don't we help them to succeed.

The Finance Director gave his own impression of how strategies
are formulated in the Trust:

> Our corporate strategies are evolved over a period of time
> through discussions between the executive directors and the
> Trust Board. In a sense our strategies are evolved through our
> management style. We have a visionary Chief Executive, a
> Medical Director who has a very cool head and knows how
> everything works, a Director of Operations who is a real go-
> getter, a good ideas person and a driver, a Personnel Director
> who is a thinker, and I, who am very task-orientated. And out
> of this we get our strategies.

The importance of the team approach was further underlined by the Director of Operations:

> Our strategy has to be very flexible. We put it together by debate amongst executive members of the Board . . . and this has all the hallmarks of people who have worked together for a long time, and trust one another, and don't take offence.

HR strategy

The following comments were made about HR strategy:

> My contribution to the HR strategy is to keep on asking the question: 'What sort of person will we need in five, eight and 10 years' time to deliver the care?' (Director of Operations)

> We have to be an organisation which can do whatever the purchasers require. So our corporate strategy has to be about preparedness, flexibility, attitude and reputation. So it's very much a personnel strategy. (Director of Human Resources)

Pilkington Optronics Limited

Background

Pilkington Optronics is engaged in the business of precision engineering, including the development and manufacture of specialised optical, mechanical, electrical and electronic equipment primarily for defence purposes.

Two major factors have affected the company: first, the contraction in the defence industry and, second, the change in government policy from cost-plus contracting to competitive tendering. This compelled the company to develop an entirely new business strategy and to carry out a comprehensive re-engineering process.

Critical success factors

Tom O'Neill, the Managing Director, stated unequivocally:

> The things that are essential to an organisation's success, any organisation, not just this one, are the people. They are the common denominator throughout the organisation.

The critical success factors for Pilkington Optronics were defined as follows:

> The one factor that drives us is technology know-how. This means we offer solutions, not products. That is really what we have to sell and it depends on people strength. (Managing Director)

> We have a vision of what we want to be and are advancing more quickly than the rest of the competition. CIM [computer-integrated manufacture] is at the heart of it. We have tackled MRPII [manufacturing requirements planning] as the first phase of CIM and this means that we are faster than our competitors and are more likely to deliver on time than them. (General Manager)

> We are characterised in the market place as a high-tech company with specific expertise in the field of optics and particularly electro-optics. We are known for the excellence of our technical solutions and the quality of our products. In the past we have been criticised for asking a premium price for high-technology products. Part of the message we are now getting across is that we can battle it out on value for money as well . . . People like working with us because they get straight answers to their questions including 'we don't know' if we really don't know. So our basic competences are high technical quality and people with the skills needed to forge good relationships with customers. (Marketing Director)

> The three critical things are price, quality and service. (Management Accountant)

Business strategy

Business strategy is stimulated and reviewed centrally by a business strategy group. The business is split into a number of sectors (three in Glasgow) and each sector submits its business plan to the strategy group. This is a simple three-page summary which describes the broad objectives of their business sector, discusses the key competitive factors affecting it and sets out specific short- to medium-term objectives which are then translated into an operating plan. The plans look at a horizon of 10 years but for practical purposes there is a rolling three-year budget. This means that besides looking at the immediate budget the two key questions asked are, as Lawrie Rumens (the General Manager) put it: 'Where are you going to be in three years' time? What are you doing now to get better?' And this, he said, 'is a very demanding discipline'.

Gordon McLean explained the approach from his point of view as Marketing Director as follows:

> The key to the business planning process is that it has to be a linked story from the top to the bottom of the company and MRPII is part of the vehicle for doing that. Our Director of Strategic Planning works with the Technical Director to involve and guide the Board on the overall strategic direction of the company. This is communicated as the strategic vision. Working from that, my role is to work with the group directors to evolve strategies for each of the businesses we have chosen to be in. These are then reviewed and agreed by the executive and a strategic development group. One of the roles of that group is to check that our activities relate to and support the strategy established by the executive. If they do not, this may not be because they are wrong, and we may have to go back and review the strategy.

The formulation of business strategy is very much a team effort. As the Managing Director said:

> I tell all the top executive people, including the Personnel and Finance Directors, that they are directors first and foremost and all must make a contribution to strategic planning.

The lead may be taken by the Managing Director and the strategic team, of which the Personnel Director is a member, but the heads of the business groups make a major and continuing contribution. The broad thrust of the strategy as a means of realising the vision is quite clear, but it is in a constant state of evolution, reacting as necessary in response to changing situations but also proactively anticipating new opportunities.

Personnel strategies

The overall approach to the formulation of personnel strategies was summarised by the Managing Director as follows:

> The main thing we have to do is to ensure that we have the right core technologies and the right competences within the company to achieve the vision and strategy.

The General Manager, Lawrie Rumens, commented:

> Within the Board one of the things that is constantly reviewed is HR strategy. We have the long-term view of the type of organisation we believe we need as a technology company and we have evolutionary plans of how we are going to get there. In the early stages we had a very strong functional organisation; our evolution process now involves the development of problem-solving teams which are set up at a high standard to encourage getting it right first time. In manufacturing we have mixed-discipline teams with a team leader and a much flatter structure than we used to have. We have two pilot projects where research and development engineers are part of the team on the shop floor with a common team leader. The eventual aim is for all engineering and manufacturing to be organised in this way. The next step is to develop product families in which business generation and sales are brought into the team as well. So the team leaders almost become general managers.

The Marketing Director, Gordon McLean, pointed out that the personnel strategy 'was clearly established in the planning process and it had hard objectives in the same way as the business strategy'.

The Personnel Director, David Roberts, explained that business strategy defines what has to be done to achieve success and that personnel strategy must complement it, bearing in mind that one of the critical success factors for the company is its ability to attract and retain the best people. Personnel strategy must help to ensure that Pilkington Optronics is a best-practice company. This implies that:

> The personnel strategy must be in line with what is best in industry and this may mean visiting four or five different companies, looking at what they are doing and taking a bit from one and a bit from another and moulding them together to form the strategy.

Rover Group Limited

Background

Rover Group Limited embraces the former three businesses of Rover Group, Land Rover and Austin Rover as a single entity. It was formerly owned by British Aerospace Ltd but is now owned by BMW. However, there has been a close link with Honda since 1979 and, as David Bower, Personnel Director, commented:

> We have learnt a great deal from that association. It has been a challenging and demanding partnership and the relationship has undoubtedly helped to inject pace in the process of change.

The quality strategy

The quality strategy is based very firmly on the vision established four years ago that 'Rover Group will be internationally renowned for extraordinary customer satisfaction'. This is supported by four key strategic thrusts:

1. Satisfy customers.
2. Move upmarket and take a more premium position in all sectors of the market place.
3. Grow in Europe and internationally to remove Rover's over-reliance on the UK market.
4. Reduce the break-even point.

John Towers, Chief Executive, emphasised the vital importance of creating a 'culture of customer satisfaction' together with the strategy for product renewal:

> Success in our business requires us to achieve a number of important objectives, but above all, we must delight customers. And if we don't do that we achieve nothing in the long term. We have achieved much in the short term in the product, financial and structural areas but they are only starting points.

Critical success factors

As stated by John Towers, the critical success factors for the business are in the areas of product engineering, manufacturing, the supplier chain and customer services.

Alan Curtis, Managing Director Product Supply (ie the whole of the product development, manufacturing and purchasing activities of Rover Group) emphasised quality as a critical success factor:

> We have to ensure that the product can be reliably manufactured every day in a volume manufacturing environment. We have to fulfil the product specification, which means having processes which are sufficiently robust and capable to guarantee that the product will turn out *every* time to the standard we expect . . . The overriding influence here is the part people play, because although we have quite a lot of technology in the manufacturing process, particularly in the metal-welding and paint processes, even in those areas people variability can be a big influence on the final quality. And in the assembly area it is almost entirely down to people.

People strategy

The Chief Executive, John Towers, explained his approach to people strategy as follows:

> The most fundamental and vital part of our people strategy is to create in Rover a sense of collective contribution to the process and business changes which move the business forward – enabling people to contribute, and providing space for them.

We were also assured by Tony Rose, Finance and Strategy Director of Rover Group, that this does not mean in any sense that financial matters continually dominate board discussions – other issues are given as much or more consideration as the need arises.

Alan Curtis, Managing Director Product Supply, emphasised:

> The people strategy, in macro terms as opposed to the personnel department strategy, is governed by the fact that we have had to accelerate our rate of progress from a company in rather serious decline in the late 1980s to one which will match world-class standards by the mid-1990s. We are trying to do in seven or eight years what it took the Japanese to do in 40. This means that we have had to outpace the rest of the competition . . . So it's been clear now for several years that the only way we will survive long-term in business is in the involvement of people, every one of the 33,000 we employ. Our whole thrust is therefore contribution from people. We've done it through a number of focused programmes, originally a total-quality programme leading into 'Rover Tomorrow', and the creation of a 'new deal' environment in which people are encouraged to make contributions without fear. We have developed mechanisms for participation including quality action teams. And we have changed our organisation to focus on process rather than on functional divides. In manufacturing in particular, we have taken away the multiple layers of management which were there to direct rather than lead.

Summing up the main thrust of the people strategy as he saw it, Graham Morris, Managing Director Rover Europe, said:

Its key feature is involvement of everyone, to get the maximum proactive and voluntary contribution from all of our people in the business. We have a policy that we all have two jobs – to do the job we are paid for and to improve that job. We have a commitment to our people to improve them as individuals, and this is by a learning process as opposed to a training process . . .

A further key part of the strategy is 'alignment' so that everyone knows what they are supposed to be doing and what the company is about and the direction it is going.

People strategies

The basis for formulating people strategies is provided by the following statements of personnel vision, mission and critical success factors which were originally established in 1990 by a Total Quality Project Group and were updated in 1993.

Vision   Success Through People – all associates willingly give their best to achieve extraordinary customer satisfaction.

Mission   To develop and facilitate the implementation of people strategies and plans to enable the company to achieve its objectives.

Critical success factors   We must:

1. **Create the culture** which provides purpose, dignity and recognition to every individual in an environment of trust which is open, safe and secure.
2. **Help the leaders lead** by empowering and supporting them in pursuit of company goals.
3. **Achieve world-class resourcing standards**, ensuring we have the right people in the right numbers with the right skills in the right place at the right time – right first time.
4. **Create continuous learning**, involving development opportunities for everyone and the sharing of best practice.
5. **Ensure company-wide understanding of the compelling business needs** by maintaining continuous dialogue.

6. **Empower individuals and teams** to achieve success through commitment, motivation, flexibility and skills development.
7. **Foster positive involvement relationships** with the broader Rover community.

The people strategy involves identifying key personnel objectives and the gaps between plans and achievements. It is linked very closely with the quality strategy achievement initiatives and the process improvement plans as expressed in quality policy statements.

The strategy is then focused on what is termed 'the vital few' which cover the macro processes, the objectives, the milestones and, importantly, the measures.

Welland Water

Background

Welland Water is a large water company operating, as pointed out by the Managing Director, 'in a monopolistic situation providing a service that is absolutely fundamental to life'. But he also stated:

> We recognise that our organisation must not abuse that situation and that we must implant in the company values that would be appropriate in a competitive environment.

He went on to say:

> We can demonstrate that the services we are giving our customers are improving dramatically, year on year . . . We have an on-going commitment to involve our customers – we were the first water company to actually prepare an annual report for them . . . We carry out frequent tracking research which shows that our customers' perceptions of us are improving, on occasions despite a contrary trend in the national water industry . . . But the critical success factor which allows all this to happen is the level of employee satisfaction and commitment we have,

because without that, we can't achieve any of the other
things. And we know about this because we get consultants
to carry out periodic employee surveys which we discuss
with everyone.

Business strategy

The Managing Director described the approach to formulating
business strategy as follows:

> Our strategic approach is very simple. It is summarised in our
> vision statement: we aim to provide the level of services our
> customers demand at a level of charges that our customers
> would see as acceptable.
>
> Our business strategies are formed essentially from top-down
> setting of the parameters and then bottom-up preparation of
> business plans in which all our people are involved. They pre-
> pare all their own business plans which reflect the top-down
> constraints, and because they are preparing them that automat-
> ically buys their commitment to them.
>
> Our best ideas for policies and strategies come from the
> people who carry out the work. We don't have people locked
> into little rooms thinking: 'What's the next strategic move for
> the business?'
>
> What you need are people who are in tune with what's hap-
> pening throughout the organisation; who are listening, talking,
> picking up all the ideas . . . What we try to do is to capture all
> that knowledge, all those initiatives, all that expertise, and
> reflect that in the way we take the business forward.
>
> I like to talk about getting values in place rather than con-
> structing strategies.

The Finance Director explained the significance of the vision
statement in developing business strategies:

> The company developed a vision statement which encom-
> passes the key forward-looking strategy over a period of time
> but without time scales having been set down. This has set the

guidelines for future initiatives and any such initiative in the
rolling five-year business plan is judged on whether it fits in
with that vision.

HR strategy

The Managing Director made the point that:

> The only HR strategy you really need is the tangible expres-
> sion of values and the implementation of values . . . Unless
> you get the HR values right you can forget all the rest.

The Finance Director commented:

> There's a lot of interaction, prior to and during the top board
> discussion which tends to be concerned with culturally based
> issues and the way we manage people.

And the Director of Operations indicated that the organisation
developed its HR strategy 'through evolution; it's an aggregation
of things that have come together, not necessarily in the right
order'.

The approach to developing HR strategy was described by the
Head of Personnel as follows:

> Our original HR strategy was developed in 1986/87. We tried
> to encompass in it the emerging values and principles that we
> felt should determine how we should conduct our business in
> terms of people.
>
> HR strategies come from the ideas we share together and the
> problems and issues that managers are working on . . . It's
> very much a team effort, working with line colleagues in
> whatever they do . . . I use electronic mail to flash ideas round
> to groups of managers and thus build up draft policy papers.
> Electronic mail is a very powerful device for getting ideas
> back rapidly.

Comments on the research findings

In all the eight organisations referred to above:

- there is a well-defined corporate or business strategy, although the extent to which it is formalised varies
- HR strategy is seen as part of the business strategy (the issue of integration will be discussed more thoroughly in Chapter 6)
- so far as we could judge, HR strategy or policy issues are of interest to *all* members of the Board (with the possible exception of Bookworld) and, contrary to popular opinion, that includes the Finance Director

Although we did not obtain a cross section of directors' opinions in the other two organisations we visited (Motorola and Albion Bank) the impression we were given was that their practices could be described as similar to those referred to above.

It is not possible to make sweeping generalisations on the basis of this limited evidence that 'everybody's doing it', although it must be said that this has not deterred other writers making equally sweeping generalisations to the effect that 'nobody's doing it'. But the research did indicate that a variety of large organisations are practising something which, according to the criteria set out in Chapter 3, could broadly be described as strategic HRM, although none of them used this phrase.

This research does not support Storey's (1993) findings. On the basis of research conducted in 1986–8 he asserted:

> A demonstrable link between business strategy and labour management practices was usually hard to establish. There was a welter of managerial initiatives but there could be little confidence that the initiatives were of a strategic character. They were often simply added on to the prevailing set of practices.

This is certainly not the case in 1994 in the 10 organisations we visited, and it is surely not unreasonable to suppose that other organisations have made progress in similar directions over the last six or seven years in response to the changing demands made on them in a recession and an increasingly competitive environment.

Indeed, other recent research such as that conducted by Guest and Hogue (1994) in 120 greenfield site companies established that, in general, they had HR strategies formally endorsed and actively supported by top management. And the research carried out by Tyson and Witcher (1994) has indicated that an approach which could broadly be described as strategic HRM is being adopted by many more organisations; although they noted that while all the 30 companies they studied had some formal strategy statements and documents, only seven of them had a formal written HR strategy document. However, we would not use the latter point as a test of whether or not strategic HRM was being practised. The organisation covered by our research where HR strategy was prob-ably the least well integrated had a written HR strategy.

What our case-study organisations have clearly demonstrated is that progress can be made in situations where they are striving to be more competitive and improve all-round organisational effective-ness. These imperatives for change are facing all organisations in the mid-1990s and there is no reason to suppose that they will be different for the rest of the decade and beyond. What is being increasingly recognised is that the strategic changes required in these circumstances can only be achieved by the formulation and implementation of integrated people strategies, which, incidentally, do not have to be given the HRM label to be regarded as strategic.

Common threads

Of course, the practices of the eight organisations discussed above varied widely in detail but, so far as the overall approach to strategic management was concerned, it is possible to detect certain common threads running through them which applied equally to the private- and public-sector organisations, with the possible exception of Bookworld. The common threads we detected are as follows:

- strong, visionary and often charismatic leadership from the top
- well-articulated missions and values, the latter often including a strong emphasis on quality and customer service (Tyson and Witcher, 1994, noted the importance their respondents attached to corporate values)
- a clearly expressed business strategy which had been implemented successfully
- a positive focus on well-understood critical success factors
- a closely related range of products or services being offered to customers
- a cohesive top management team
- a personnel/HR director who played an active part in discussing corporate/business issues as well as making an effective and corporate/business-orientated contribution on HR matters.

5

Strategic HRM in Action – the content of HR strategies

The rhetoric behind the concepts of strategic management, HRM and strategic HRM has an inspiring ring about it but does anything actually happen? And if so, what does it look like? Process is important, but content and action are also required. We assumed that the basis of any approach an organisation used to develop and implement HR strategies would be the philosophy of influential members of the top team on managing people. We examined the content and programmes of the organisations covered by our research to identify what was contained in their HR strategies and how they were implementing them. This was done under the headings of:

- macro, corporate issues such as vision and mission, organisation, performance, quality and customer care, commitment, and the introduction of new technology
- the more specific HR strategy areas of resourcing, learning, development and training, reward and employee relations

Philosophy on managing people

The philosophy on managing people is a broad strategic issue associated with management style, and it is one which may never be articulated and often remains on a 'taken for granted' basis like other manifestations of corporate culture. The philosophy may lead to a 'hard HRM' or a 'soft HRM' approach as described in Chapter 2, page 29).

But to adapt a common if somewhat inadequate definition of corporate culture, strategic HRM is about 'the way things should be done around here in the future'. Questions can be asked about the traditional or underlying philosophy, the extent to which it is still relevant and the directions in which it might usefully change.

86

The philosophy of the Managing Director of Megastores on managing people was expressed as follows:

> There is immense strength and talent in any body of people numbering 50,000 and we are negligent if we don't tap that resource as far as we possibly can.
>
> The contribution of our managers to added value is immense because they are people managers . . . They are not managing systems, they are not managing machinery and they are not managing shops – you can't manage a shop, you manage people within a shop.
>
> I have always advocated the employment of the highest calibre of people we can find, and I think we've got that . . . We are in the vanguard of retailing. Our net profit to sales ratio is about the highest in the high street and in profit terms we are growing at a faster rate than the market. The biggest challenge will be to maintain that competitive advantage and to do that we need to maintain and continue to attract very high-calibre people.

The Operations Director of Morton Healthcare Trust said: 'Ours is a success-orientated approach . . . What we aim to do is to create an environment in which people are successful.'

The Chief Executive of Rover Group, John Towers, expresses his philosophy as follows:

> The only way anything happens in any business, large or small, is through the people in the business. If you have got policies and processes in place which allow them to make their contribution in a more forceful and highly motivated way, then you are going to have a wonderfully run business. That's the difference. At one time the role of personnel was to get people to do what they were supposed to do: the future role of personnel is much more about stretching the limits of what people are actually capable of doing.

Rover Group has questioned the whole basis upon which they were organised. As David Bower, Personnel Director put it:

> Over the past four years there has been a shift in emphasis from traditional hierarchical functional organisation to processes

and company culture. Far less importance is now placed on
the organisation chart of names in boxes and far more on
process and network analysis and leadership style.

He also commented:

Our strategy is to stimulate changes on a broad front aimed
ultimately at achieving competitive advantage through the
efforts of our people. In an industry of fast followers, those
who learn quickest will be the winners.

Ultimately, therefore, the philosophy on managing people will
depend upon the extent to which top management *really* believes in
'success through people'.

Corporate issues

Vision and mission

In the broadest terms strategic HRM is concerned with the people
implications of top management's vision of the future of the organisation and the mission it is there to fulfil. HR strategies, like those
of all the other functions, are there to support the realisation of the
vision and mission of the organisation and the achievement of its
goals.

At ABC Distribution the vision is that the organisation will be the
'premier quality distribution business, acknowledged by its customers, its employees and the public as commercially successful,
competitive, socially and environmentally responsible through its
commitment to quality, reliability and value'. This vision influences
everything that the organisation sets out to achieve.

The vision of Loamshire Council is that it will 'establish and
maintain excellent services, management and value and in so doing
will seek constantly to adapt and develop to make a significant
contribution to people's lives'. These aspirations are underpinned
by a management strategy based on a set of values on caring for

customers, employees and the environment; encouraging openness and trust, good communications and positive thinking; and on working together to enhance the effectiveness of its services, providing high quality and 'value for money'.

David Roberts, Personnel Director at Pilkington Optronics, made the following comment about vision and strategy:

> The first thing is that the organisation has to know is where it is going. That is why it needs a vision. It has to know why it exists and who its customers are. This leads to the development of strategies which in turn lead to action plans. The plans follow three lanes: systems, processes and people.

Two of the other functional directors at Pilkington Optronics commented on the significance of vision and a sense of purpose or mission:

> I would put it in a single word, which is vision. If you can create a vision and communicate it to people you can release a colossal current of energy . . . Communication and vision means education and training and I am one of the operational guys who believe that whatever you are currently spending on education and training you start by doubling it. (Lawrie Rumens, General Manager)

> What contributes most to success is a clear sense of purpose and definition of where you are trying to get to. Unless you have a top team with a clear and unified understanding of purpose and direction it can be difficult to cascade it throughout the organisation. (Gordon McLean, Marketing Director)

In Rover Group, for example, the vision is that the company 'will be internationally renowned for extraordinary customer satisfaction'. This feeds directly into the total quality improvement (TQI) strategy as described later in this chapter.

The Managing Director of Welland Water commented:

> We look at our vision for the company and we say: 'How do we maximise the contribution that our people can make to achieving that vision?'

Organisation

HR strategy may address such issues as:

- structure
- team working
- downsizing

Structure   The Managing Director of ABC Distribution said:

> I do not see any difference between the HR strategy and the
> business strategy on organisation because we evolve our
> organisation to reflect where the business is going.

Referring to what is in effect an overall strategy of achieving
change in a fast-moving business environment, the Chief Executive
of Bookworld described how an organisation review is being
tackled:

> HR has made a major input into the review, acting as one of
> the catalysts. The other catalysts have been outside consul-
> tants. But the review is answerable to me because I tried to get
> people to reorganise themselves and of course they couldn't
> do it because they couldn't agree amongst themselves.

And as the Managing Director of Megastores said, 'You cannot
fully maximise business opportunities unless you have the proper
management structure to create them.'

Rover Group provides a good example of a strategic approach
to organisation management. In 1991 the traditional functional
manufacturing and engineering organisation was abandoned and
replaced by one based on six business units covering the various
product lines. The transition was achieved by a review of organisation, processes and business culture. The review's key objective
was to define the fundamental operating principles for the Rover of
tomorrow. Initially, the top 30 or so managers of the manufacturing
and engineering functions set about this task, focusing on principles
relating to culture, processes and organisation. The key principles
were concerned with:

Processes

- added value
- minimum interfaces
- suitable time horizons
- short cycles
- best practice related
- involvement

Culture

- leadership by leaders
- openness and honesty
- team working
- learning environment
- people orientation
- business-wide application

Organisation

- business emphasis
- broad roles
- product and process focus
- 'Polo' principle (no large central organisation)
- flat organisation
- maximum delegation of authority

What became apparent in the review was that discussion on organisation principles was exhausted far more quickly than that on processes or culture, and that it was on the latter two issues that a rich seam of change potential was identified. Having created the basis for a 'new culture' the challenge has been to harness the potential of all employees and to win their maximum contribution.

The manufacturing organisation has been under review since 1988. Employee attitude surveys revealed many important issues. Most employees did not feel that the best use was made of their talents or that they were given sufficient challenge in their jobs; they were not particularly involved in problem solving, did not enjoy a relationship of mutual trust with their boss, did not have clear opportunities to develop themselves and did not receive recognition for contribution or achievement. Creating an organisation structure which responded to these concerns became a major objective. Since then the traditional management hierarchy has been transformed. Eleven layers of manufacturing organisation have been reduced to six in organisational units of between 3,000 and 10,000 people. The traditional roles of the production superintendent and foreman have been eliminated and a new structure established in which the team leader takes on a new, key role. The teams have responsibility not only for production, but also for housekeeping, continuous improvement of processes/products, quality control and inventories. The team leader has responsibility for these activities but not for disciplinary issues.

One of the distinguishing features of the Rover 'lean organisation' is the level of responsibility devolved to shop-floor direct workers and the lower incidence of middle managers and indirect workers. This requires personal development of the individual employee to provide the broader range of personal skills and leadership. Rover Learning Business, as described later in this chapter, was established to focus on this issue.

Team working   At Pilkington Optronics the background to the work on teambuilding was the demolition of traditional hierarchies over the last two or three years. In manufacturing and engineering there are never more than three layers between team members and the director. In 80 per cent of the engineering teams there are now only two layers – the Team Manager and the Engineering Manager. It is believed that these changes have had far-reaching effects on flexibility and performance and have contributed significantly to the achievement of better co-ordination in manufacturing and engineering.

At Motorola a strategy for developing teamwork forms an important part of the HR strategy. As the HR Director explained, team development and training is an important contribution which the

HR function makes to the business. The initial training emphasises the concept of total customer satisfaction which automatically includes internal as well as external customers. People are asked to discuss the projects they are working on and if they have problems, they are encouraged to get a team of people to work with them to push the project forward. When a group of people does get together they identify what additional skills they need and training on team dynamics and teambuilding is provided.

Downsizing   It was evident that in common with many other organisations in the mid-1990s, a number of the organisations we visited were 'downsizing' – frequent references were made to the need to develop leaner organisations and in some cases this has for a time dominated HR strategy. Two interesting comments were made on this issue:

> We've never been about downsizing, we've been about cost reduction. (Managing Director, Megastores)

> Our strategy is always to manage more work with the same people rather than to have fewer people. (Chief Executive, Bookworld)

But downsizing is a strategic issue in a number of the organisations we visited, and as one personnel director put it: 'When you are going through major downsizing processes you have to be very conscious of what the needs of the people are.' It was also emphasised to us by a number of chief executives and directors that HR had a vital role in managing the changes required and maintaining good relationships with the trade unions during the process.

Performance

A performance strategy will be based on an analysis of the critical success factors and the performance levels reached in relation to them. Steps can then be agreed to improve performance by training, development, reorganisation, the development of performance management processes, some form of business process re-engineering, or simply 'taking cost out of the business'. This is how the latter aspect of strategy works in one of the key divisions of ABC Distribution as described by the Managing Director:

> We know that over the next three years we have to take more than £10 million worth of cost out of the business. So our Personnel Director sits down with the business head of the division and they identify the areas we need to focus on. It could be productivity enhancement, it could be changing work practices, it could be making sure that we have no anomalies round the depots in terms of payment, it could even be taking tea breaks out. A three-year strategy is agreed, targets are set and then they get on with it.

The Chief Executive of Bookworld had this to say about their performance management system:

> We have developed schemes in which clear objectives are set for everyone, not just managers, and they are measured against them. But three or four years on it's getting very difficult to think of things to say. How do you tell someone who was excellent last year that they are not quite so excellent this year? And then you get the reply, 'I did exactly what I did last year, so why aren't I excellent this year?' So you say: 'Well everybody else has caught up with you, so everybody's excellent, and you are not better than they are, so you're average!' . . . We have found that all these HR things have a product life cycle, just like products in the marketing world, and the life cycle gets shorter over the years. Things used to last six or seven years, now they last three or four before they begin to creak and you have to introduce something else.

The approach at Loamshire Council was described by the Director of Personnel as follows:

> We have a general strategy of performance measurement and management from which grew our performance appraisal system, which has worked extremely well . . . We spent a lot of time ensuring that people understood that this was a development process and it was about not just their competence, but also the ability of the organisation to achieve what it wants to achieve.

The strategy for improving performance at Megastores involves the use of a performance management system which was introduced, as the Director of Personnel explained, 'because we didn't have any mechanism through which we could run the business through the people'. He went on to say: 'Line management own it totally. It's not a personnel system, it's a line management system for running the business.' He also made the following comments on performance strategies:

> We set out to understand the differences between successful and less successful performance within the organisation and we call those our competency frameworks . . . By developing these frameworks we have educated the whole of our line management throughout the organisation into how to think about their people in a much wider sense.

> Our key HR strategy question is: 'How do we actually get the people to deliver what the business requires?'

Performance improvement may involve dealing with people who are judged to be incompetent. This is how the Chief Executive of Morton Healthcare Trust explained his approach:

> We introduced a Trust policy that if somebody isn't competent to do their job they should be found a job at which they are competent. Because to some extent if somebody's in a job they're not able to do, that's a fault of the service rather than the individual. If you're running a cricket side and you put a bowler on and he can't bowl, it's not his fault he can't bowl, it's your fault for asking him to do something he couldn't do.

The process of performance improvement could mean, as Pilkington Optronics' Marketing Director put it, 'going through a lot of effort to ensure that we have the correct level of performance in what we do and underpinning this with financial and commercial stability'.

Pilkington Optronics has become one of the most quoted examples of successful performance improvement through business process re-engineering in the UK (although that is not what it was called at the time). The exercise took the form of a functional analysis process, which, as described by David Roberts, was carried out as in Figure 5.1.

Figure 5.1
Methodology of occupational analysis to meet the company's business needs

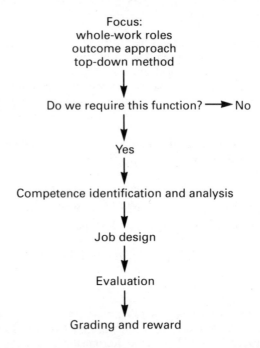

Focus:
whole-work roles
outcome approach
top-down method
↓
Do we require this function? ⟶ No
↓
Yes
↓
Competence identification and analysis
↓
Job design
↓
Evaluation
↓
Grading and reward

This could be described as business process re-engineering with people in mind.

At Welland Water, the Head of Personnel thought that:

> Performance improvement lies not so much in creating the hard issues at the bottom line but on creating an environment within which people will accept change and co-operate in different methods of working. And I believe our partnership does create such an environment, one in which we can manage change successfully and which encourages people to accept new responsibilities and acquire new skills.

The majority of the organisations we visited had installed or were installing performance-management systems in which the emphasis is on performance improvement and development and not reward. In accordance with best practice on performance appraisal, the Rover scheme emphasises the new priorities of involvement, team-work and self-development as well as more standard measures. Rover has also introduced upward appraisal in some areas at management level.

Quality and customer care

Quality, which in essence means customer satisfaction, is generally recognised today as the key to the achievement of competitive advantage. Innovation and cost reduction are still important but they are to no avail if customers ultimately reject the product because it does not meet their expectations.

Quality is achieved through people and, in accordance with a basic HRM principle, investment in people is a prerequisite for achieving high quality standards. This is the bedrock of Mega-store's approach to people management.

A strategy for total quality is a true HRM strategy in the sense that it is owned and delivered by management. It should therefore be built into their business strategy as it is, for example, at Rover, Pilkington Optronics and Motorola.

At ABC Distribution, as the Personnel Director mentioned that 'our policy is to move toward TQM using BS 5750 as a stepping stone'.

The Chief Executive of Loamshire Council said:

> We have a performance appraisal system and one area that we are particularly keen should be dealt with as part of that process is the contribution of the individual to our customer-care standards.

The HR Director of Motorola described it as a 'quality-driven' company, and at Albion Bank the focus is very much on service – on meeting the demands of customers for more sophisticated banking.

At Pilkington Optronics, David Roberts stated that in pursuit of their goal of world-class performance, personnel strategy must help to ensure that they are a best-practice company. An important aspect of this strategy 'is to educate everyone to build quality into every job, aiming to convey to people that if you get it right first time you will be saving a lot of unnecessary work'.

Total Quality Improvement at Rover Group   David Bower at Rover emphasises that:

> Total quality improvement (TQI) in Rover Group is no longer seen as a 'programme' but is at the heart of our corporate philosophy of management. It exercises a strong and increasing influence on day-to-day activities at all levels within the company.

The whole concept of 'process understanding' within total quality improvement forms an important part of the TQI strategy. As Alan Curtis explained, the first major total quality improvement programme focused initially on awareness and the individual's contribution. This took place from 1987 until 1991, and, as the then Personnel Director, he was its instigator and first champion. But two years into the programme a picture emerged, as he put it 'of a lot of arrows which represented activity, but the arrows were not lined up – they all appeared in a fairly random fashion'. So quality action teams were set up which allowed groups of people to solve far more difficult problems in a co-ordinated way.

It was then recognised that a strategy for continuous improvement required the company to concentrate on processes. The following list of business processes was created by consensus activity:

- product improvement
- new product introduction
- logistics
- sales/distribution service
- manufacture
- maintenance
- business planning

- corporate learning
- management of people.

As Alan Curtis said:

> Knowing that there were only a million things to work on, we appreciated that there had to be a widespread involvement of people in the delivery of quality, it couldn't just be a management-driven activity . . . So the ownership of processes lies in the hands of people in their work areas – and BS5750 has been used as a means of getting definition and ownership of processes in the places where the work gets done.

For each of the nine business processes, over 700 stakeholders (owners, suppliers and customers) were involved in defining business process milestones over a five-year period (1990–5) and a quality strategy milestone chart was produced. Action was then taken to quantify the achievement goal for each milestone. For example, the achievement of a world, best-in-class standard in a particular year requires a definition of what that standard will be by then. To derive this, benchmarking is used to establish current best-in-class and the rate at which people are travelling, and the achievement goals are extrapolated from this data.

The output is a list of goals for achievement year by year for each process, and this is monitored by the Group Quality Council. Responsibility for the delivery of the goals is cascaded into the twelve strategic projects and annual management action plans throughout the company. This produces alignment between the quality strategy and the Rover Group vision.

Commitment

Commitment refers to the relative strength of the individual's identification with, and involvement in, a particular organisation and the extent to which they accept its values and focus their efforts on achieving its goals. The concept plays an important part in HRM philosophy. Guest (1987) has indicated that HRM policies are designed to 'maximise organisational integration, employee commitment, flexibility and quality of work'.

As stated by Gordon McLean of Pilkington Optronics the 'need for rapid change at the strategic level means taking the workforce with you'.

Graham Morris, Managing Director, Rover Europe said that a key part of their strategy 'is alignment, so that everyone knows what they are supposed to be doing, and what the company is about, and the direction'.

Commitment strategies at both Pilkington Optronics and Rover have been implemented through company-wide processes of involvement and communication.

Introducing new technology

A fundamental and pervading re-engineering strategy, incorporating the extensive use of computer technology, has been established in Pilkington Optronics to achieve the key aims of the financial and marketing aspects of the business strategy. This is seen as a vastly improved method of managing the business as a whole and getting things right first time rather than simply introducing some smarter techniques for processing and using data to plan and control manufacturing.

The starting point for the re-engineering process was the introduction of MRPII (Manufacturing Resource Planning). This is a computer-based system designed to manage all the resources of a manufacturing organisation. It acts as a planning and scheduling system, linking manufacturing with the sales and finance departments and providing tools for joint decision-making among all three departments.

This is now being followed up by the development of CIM (computer integrated manufacturing). This uses computer technology to integrate all the business processes in a manufacturing company. These include design, production engineering, production planning, manufacturing, material handling, inventory control, purchasing, cost accounting and distribution. CIM provides for the systems which manage and control these processes to exchange information with one another. It is the ultimate development of computer-aided design and computer-aided manufacturing (CADCAM) systems in association with computerised production and process planning and control systems. However, CIM is also very much about the integration of people and technology and linking key business processes to other key business functions.

As the General Manager, Lawrie Rumens pointed out, the introduction of CIM takes a lot of time and effort and involves four phases:

1. **Co-ordination** – getting the act together
2. **Process control** – getting things right first time
3. **Process improvement** – systematising everything to a computer base
4. **System integration** – putting the whole system together on an organisation-wide basis

The personnel function is very much a partner with engineering and manufacturing in the strategy for introducing CIM. At board level the Personnel Director, David Roberts participates in the development of the CIM strategy and the joint evaluation of the people considerations. At the implementation level, Jackie Anderson, the Personnel Manager at Glasgow, is an active member of the CIM project team. Amongst many other activities, this has involved working with the Engineering Manager in developing the Advanced Operations Strategy by drawing up competence maps showing for each activity the competences available now and what will be needed in five years' time. These will form the basis for long-term operational resourcing and training/development plans.

Questioned about the management of major technological change, the Managing Director of Megastores observed that:

> It is difficult to be specific but if you have an attitude and approach to what might be described as open government, involvement, quality teams, debate and discussion, then these things [ie technological change] happen without an immense amount of trauma, frankly. We are in the vanguard of retail technology, retail engineering as it is now called, and we've achieved that without major disruption, major concern.

Specific HR strategies

Resourcing

HRM is fundamentally about matching human resources to the strategic and operational needs of the organisation and ensuring the full utilisation of those resources. It is concerned not only with obtaining and keeping the number and quality of staff required but also with selecting and promoting people who 'fit' the culture and the strategic requirements of the organisation.

At ABC Distribution the Director of Personnel remarked that 'expansion is basically about having the right people' and this was underlined by the Director of Network Business when he said:

> There are a number of influences on the human resource strategy. The primary one is the business strategy and we specifically look at the implications of the business strategy on the types and qualities of managers and people that we'll need. Then it becomes an HR responsibility to help us meet these requirements.

On this aspect of strategy, the Managing Director of Megastores commented: 'I have always advocated the employment of the highest calibre of people we can find, and I think we've got that.' At Megastores this belief was backed up by the extensive use of competency frameworks as a basis for getting the right quality of people, making judgements about their performance and developing them.

The Personnel Director of Pilkington Optronics, David Roberts, was clear that 'the HR strategy is basically built around compet- ences'. Competence analysis is related to the core or distinctive com- petences – this involves competence profiling and 'competence mapping' (long-range forecasts of competence requirements). It is used to determine people requirements, devise plans for training and developing them and to produce the information required for succes- sion planning. It also provides the basis for job evaluation, which, as he said 'is at the heart of the whole competence-driven strategy'. The analysis started from a definition of the core competences of the company and this has been broken down into jobs. He explained that five years ago they had 250 different job titles. The first cut of job evaluation suggested that there were 35, the second cut will bring it down to about 25.

Learning, training and development

HR strategy can address the question of the extent to which it is desirable or possible for the enterprise to become a 'learning organisation'. These are typical 'buzz words' in the HRM vocabulary but the reality at Rover is that corporate learning has been identified as one of the nine key business processes within the overarching corporate quality strategy. Corporate learning is defined by Rover as the process by which the business identifies, acquires, disseminates, retains, shares and updates best practice. The development of this process has been organised and stimulated largely through Rover Learning Business (RLB).

RLB is a 'business within the business'. It has its own Chairman, Managing Director, Executive Committee and Board of Governors. Its primary aim is to provide a top-quality learning and development service to all employees as customers, regardless of geography and with equal opportunity. It is committed to providing assistance to everyone wishing to develop themselves. It attempts to change the emphasis from 'training', which most people still regard as having something done to them, to 'learning' – doing something for themselves. Its first Chairman was Sir Graham Day, who accepted the role when he was also Chairman of the Rover Group. This helped, almost at a stroke, to raise the profile of learning and development within the organisation and caused line management to reassess the importance of learning at both a personal and a business level.

In addition to personal learning and development, a corporate learning database has been created. This allows for and encourages the capture of key learning points in all business activities. It can be accessed readily and its development is being championed by members of RLB's Executive Committee.

The emphasis within RLB's title on the word 'learning' was

intentional. It was designed to bring about a switch of emphasis to enable self-development and acceptance of responsibility for learning by the individuals and their line managers to be the way forward rather than the traditional route of waiting to be trained. The intention has been to establish a more populist approach to learning and development, emphasising that careers can be pursued, not only by a relatively small band of professional and managerial employees, but also by any employee who is motivated to take up the challenge. The Personnel Mission Statement sets out the objectives for Rover to create that kind of learning environment. More traditional training is still carried out within the company and David Bower believes that the two approaches live very comfortably together.

At Pilkington Optronics the aim is to achieve 'world-class' standards in its personnel strategies and practices and, flowing naturally from this imperative, training and development is treated as a major investment and given high priority. The Managing Director is quite clear that 'training is the key to changing people, and if you think training is expensive, try ignorance'. And the Personnel Director made the point that:

> In most companies when money is hard to get one of the first things cut is the training and development budget. In this company that has not been the case and this year we will spend well over £1 million in training and development on this site (ie over £1,500 per employee). The reason for this is that the Executive realise that if we are going to have the workforce with the skills and technology they need to do the job, we have *got* to train and develop them, and that takes money.

A number of the organisations we visited are involved in Investing in People (IIP), including Rover, Pilkington Optronics and Megastores. They see it as a valuable adjunct to their training and development strategies. The Managing Director of Megastores' comment on training was: 'I am not sure training is a good word. I've never liked it . . . it's education. You train dogs, you educate people.' And the Finance Director felt that:

> A key success factor for us has undoubtedly been the amount of time and effort that we put into the training and management of staff, although there's an awful lot more we can do. We are at the leading edge in staff development. We were the first retailer into NVQs, the first to win the IIP award.

Reward

As the Director of Stores at Megastores put it:

> The only way you are going to deliver added value to customers is by having the best staff and you've got to reward them accordingly . . . And this is a further role for personnel in advancing best practice in conditions of employment within what the business can afford, because if they are not the champions, who is?

Employee relations

An HRM approach to employee relations is characterised by:

- a belief that employees should be managed as efficiently and tightly as any other resource in order to maximise added value
- a drive towards achieving competitive advantage by gaining commitment through intensive training and indoctrination programmes. This is coupled with a belief in the benefits of 'mutuality' – a shared interest in corporate success, ie a unitarist philosophy
- the organisation of complementary forms of communication, such as team briefing, alongside traditional collective bargaining – ie approaching employees directly as individuals or in groups rather than through their representatives
- the use of employee involvement techniques such as quality circles or improvement groups
- a continuous drive for quality – total quality management
- increased flexibility in working arrangements to provide for the more cost-effective use of human resources
- emphasis on teamwork

Trade union strategies

Contrary to the opinion of some people, HRM is not necessarily anti-union, and in all the unionised organisations we covered, including Loamshire Council, ABC Distribution, Albion Bank, Megastores, Pilkington Optronics, Rover Group, Welland Water and Morton Healthcare Trust, the strategy was to work with the unions, not against them – in effect, to take them into partnership.

However, much of what was being done in the manufacturing organisations we visited conformed broadly to the characteristics of the HRM approach summarised above, and this was clearly based on a deliberate and clearly articulated employee-relations strategy.

None of the organisations covered by our research had withdrawn union recognition. This is in line with the findings of recent research (not yet published) involving 27 organisations carried out by Professor Gennard and Dr Kelly and of the Strathclyde Business School. This revealed that none of the personnel directors had withdrawn trade union recognition and, with one possible exception, they had all involved unions in their change strategies. The unions were, on the whole highly co-operative, recognising that in the 1990s improved performance was necessary to achieve mutual benefit. One convenor called this the 'mutuality principle'.

The strategy generally in the organisations we visited is to develop a partnership approach with the trade unions. This is seen as the only means by which the inevitable changes that will continue to take place in their industries can be managed. These changes are, of course, often associated with strategies for developing a leaner organisation – euphemistically referred to as downsizing or even 'rightsizing'. All the personnel directors we met knew that one of their key functions was to plan and manage the process in a way which minimises the painful consequences for people and wins the understanding and agreement of the unions, so far as this is possible.

The approach adopted by some of these organisations to their industrial relations and trade union strategies is described below.

Loamshire Council   A very positive message was delivered by the Chief Executive of Loamshire Council:

> I doubt you will go anywhere and find a better set of relation-
> ships in an organisation between its management leaders and
> the trade unions than you would find here . . . We value the
> contribution of the trade unions; we have been blessed with
> trade union leaders here for many years who have acted in the
> best interests both of the employees and the organisation and
> have taken a truly corporate view of their role. I can't speak
> too highly of the trade unions, the contribution they have
> made.

Morton Healthcare Trust   At Morton Healthcare Trust the Director of Human Resources said:

> We aren't in the business of negotiating. That isn't as we see it
> the role of the unions. We'd much rather they joined us in
> trying to make this place work, and they have got something
> they can contribute.

Pilkington Optronics   The industrial relations strategies at Pilkington Optronics are designed to develop trusting relationships with
officials and therefore allow for full consultation with the unions on
matters of mutual concern. As Jane Pickard (1993) has reported of
Pilkington Optronics: 'Both sides now see themselves as partners
with a mutual interest in furthering the success of the enterprise and
maintaining a satisfied workforce.'

Rover Group   At Rover Group the industrial relations strategy is
to develop positive relationships with the trade unions so that they
can make a contribution. In fact, as Alan Curtis commented, 'one
of our interests at the moment is creating a new role for trade union
representatives in the company rather than leaving them just
stranded'.
Against a background of new products and a more open culture
encouraging individual development and involvement in the business, it became quite clear that the terms and conditions of
employment were no longer appropriate. It was recognised that in

accordance with best practice it was necessary to undertake whole-
sale changes in the contractual obligations with employees. Application of these ideas was therefore sought in Rover Tomorrow, the
New Deal. As David Bower comments, 'it was no surprise that
such a radical change, in which no financial incentive was offered,
only received a very marginal vote in favour of acceptance. But the
employees' decision was positive and so the New Deal conditions
have operated since April 1992.' Briefly, these are:

- no clocking
- single-status terms and conditions
- removal of separate hourly-paid and staff grade structures –
  existing separate salary and hourly paid grading structures will
  be merged into a single scheme based on a reduced number of
  occupation classifications
- security of employment – employees who want to work for
  Rover will be able to stay with Rover. Necessary reductions in
  manpower will be achieved with the co-operation of employees
  through retraining, redeployment, natural wastage, voluntary
  redundancy and early retirement programmes. In the past four
  years over 10,000 employees have left the company, over 5,000
  since the New Deal agreement
- Team working – there will be a maximum devolution of
  authority and accountability, and teams will be responsible for
  the quality of their work, continuous improvement, routine maintenance and work allocation. Employees will be expected to par-
  ticipate in discussion groups, quality action teams, the
  suggestion scheme and other activities continuously to improve
  processes and performance
- working environment – everyone will work together to ensure
  the best possible working environment
- training and development – opportunities will be available to
  everyone to develop themselves to their full potential
- trade union representation – a single Joint Negotiating Committee will be established representing all recognised trade
  unions

Involvement and participation strategies

At ABC Distribution there is a strategy for getting increased involvement and this is being achieved through leadership training. As the Personnel Director said:

> We are getting our managers to change their style so that they ask employees to contribute more by making suggestions on how things can be improved.

At Rover, as Graham Morris explained, the key feature of their people strategy is 'involvement of everyone, to get the maximum proactive and voluntary contribution from all of our people in the business'. The involvement of Rover Group employees has been achieved through the suggestion scheme and discussion groups, quality action teams and workshops. Nearly 40 per cent of employees put forward their ideas through the suggestion scheme in both 1989 and 1990, giving almost 30,000 valuable contributions. In 1991, 70 per cent participated, and in 1992 and 1993 the suggestion rate (suggestions per year divided by the number of employees) averaged almost 100%. Well over 150 discussion groups (Rover's name for quality circles) are in operation and additionally, 500 management-led quality action teams. As David Bower said, this means that over 25,000 employees are freely, willingly and enthusiastically contributing their ideas in some formal way, as well as those already treating such inputs as part of the job.

Welland Water has a 'partnership' strategy which was described by their Director of Operations as follows:

> Our policy of partnership with our people says that we need to run the organisation as an informal team whose members have common objectives . . . We talked a lot with people about what we wanted the HR culture to be and we developed a partnership (Partnership One). We're now in the middle of Partnership Two which sets the agenda on what we are offering our people as a business and what we expect in return. We want to give our people stability and security. And we want them to focus on doing things for the organisation which will make our shareholders and customers happy. We ask for flexibility and offer the training.

Challenges

We asked a number of chief executives, personnel and other directors what they thought were the main challenges facing their organisations over the next five years and what HR changes would be
required to face these challenges. The following is a selection of
their replies which illustrate the sort of issues which are currently
concerning a fairly typical cross section of UK organisations:

> The most important challenges for us in the next five years are
> achieving sustained growth, developing new products and ser-
> vices and providing added value. The HR role is to contribute
> to the achievement of these business aims at a general level
> and then to translate the effects of these strategies into the spe-
> cific requirements that HR has to deliver. And these come
> down to management succession, quality, talent management,
> training – those sort of areas. (Managing Director, ABC Dis-
> tribution)

> The most important issue is growth and managing that
> growth. We will have to look at our management style, the
> need for flatter structures and more flexible arrangements, the
> need to be more responsive, which means involving the whole
> of the workforce and defining exactly what we mean by total
> quality and sharing that with our workforce . . . Then we have
> to pick a good idea up, run with it, and before you've finished
> another good idea comes up and you have to run with that too.
> (Personnel Director, ABC Distribution)

> We have a problem that too many people work in isolation . . .
> They have a tendency to say: 'Yeah, but that's my bit, I'm
> doing my bit, my best for marketing or finance or whatever'
> while completely ignoring what's best for the business. We've
> got to look at the structure in a way that will somehow cut
> down these barriers and HR must play a part in that. (Chief
> Executive, Bookworld)

> The overriding issue is managing change effectively because
> whatever happens, there is going to be a massive change over
> the next five years . . . HR must be able to respond to the
> changes that are coming . . . One of our outstanding areas for
> improvement is the process of translating corporate and other

strategies right down through the organisation to individual level. (Chief Executive, Loamshire Council)

The massive change will be the restructuring of local government, if it happens. It will be like starting a very new organisation on a very large scale, but probably more difficult because you have cultures and practices in place which are going to need to be developed into something different, with a new vision and different values. The other huge challenge is compulsory competitive tendering for professional services and the ability to work as a trading market – that's an enormous culture shock. (Director of Personnel, Loamshire Council)

The biggest challenge will be to maintain our competitive advantage. To do that we need to continue to attract very high-quality people and they will need to be motivated, need to be well led, need to be encouraged to be innovative. (Managing Director, Megastores)

Our biggest challenge is that we must continually differentiate ourselves in the face of potential increased competition. (Director of Central Marketing, Megastores)

The biggest challenge will be the changing nature of work. To get growth in a competitive environment we are going to have to improve those people who face the customers. We've got to have a competitive edge. Getting the right people in, training them and retaining these very valuable people will be a major challenge in the future. (Director of Personnel, Megastores)

We have two opposite requirements: we need to have more and more generalists with maximum flexibility but we also need greater and greater specialisation to improve health care. And these form substantial challenges for personnel. (Chief Executive, Morton Healthcare Trust)

We will need to be continually examining the configuration of our workforce, the profile of skills . . . We've got to have people who are happy with flexibility . . . And the other theme is that individuals are going to become more important, and the workforce has got to be seen as 6,000 individuals, rather than lots of anonymous workers. Because there's a lot of ingenuity wasted there. (Director of Human Resources, Morton Healthcare Trust)

The challenge is that of constantly changing the nature of the
company as business needs arise, and one of the main elements of that is playing to people's strengths. (Personnel
Director, Pilkington Optronics)

The big challenge is how do you find ways of rewarding
people and giving them status for the job they have to do as
you develop flatter and flatter management structures. (General Manager, Pilkington Optronics)

We're having to meet enormous challenges in controlling
operating costs and maximising efficiency. We have to deliver
very specific outputs to our customers in terms of further
improving the level of services and meeting ever-increasing
customer aspirations . . . We will meet these challenges
through our HR policies and values. We will go beyond
empowerment – a word which implies that someone is still
making a conscious act of empowerment – to a situation
where our people can manage themselves totally . . . and we
will break down the traditional hierarchies. (Managing
Director, Welland Water)

The biggest challenge will be to continue to reduce our operating costs and meet the ever-increasing quality standards.
(Head of Personnel, Welland Water)

Exciting developments

One of the questions we asked was: 'What is the most exciting HR
initiative that you are working on at the moment?' The following
selection of replies indicates what sort of issues are concerning a
number of fairly typical organisations:

- **ABC Distribution** – empowerment, leadership, management
  succession, total quality management
- **Bookworld** – reorganisation
- **Loamshire Council** – a comprehensive review of staff morale,
  IIP
- **Megastores** – training (including 'competitive advantage'

training), driving behaviours through a more sophisticated reward system

- **Morton Healthcare Trust** – the removal of old-fashioned hierarchical management, letting people run their own affairs
- **Motorola** – getting ownership and expanding the roles of people from the traditional narrow roles to much broader roles
- **Rover Group** – maximising people's skills and involvement in the business
- **Welland Water** – the development of values, the freeing-up of people and the manifestation of it actually happening; our partnership attitude to people.

The interesting thing about these comments is that they mainly focus on broad strategic issues rather than on the development and introduction of specific personnel programmes or techniques, although there were, of course, a number of HR programmes that were designed directly to support strategy. The Director of Central Marketing at Megastores gave an example:

> An exciting HR initiative right now is what we call 'competitive advantage training', which is a training technique that we are currently developing and using to enable us to respond better to our customers by recognising their real needs through the language patterns they use. It is a research technique that helps us to understand our customers better and can be developed into training modules [on interpersonal and communication skills] . . . We have used it in a number of stores already and the results are quite encouraging – we are already beginning to see some impact.

In the next chapter we examine approaches to integration and achieving coherence and consider the impact of strategic HRM on organisational performance. We then summarise the key lessons from our research on strategic HRM in action.

6

Strategic HRM in Action – integration, coherence and impact

Integration

The integration of HR and business strategies is seen by some comentators as a main distinguishing feature of strategic HRM. Doubts have been cast on the extent to which such integration does take place, often on the grounds that integration is not an issue when there are no corporate strategies. This was not the case in any of the organisations we visited and in all but two of them the HR strategies, in Walker's (1992) terms, were fully integrated, while the two exceptions (ABC Distribution and Bookworld) were 'aligned'. In fact, ABC Distribution was moving rapidly towards becoming a fully integrated company.

Achieving integration

As the Managing Director of ABC Distribution pointed out:

> Our HR strategy has to respond to our business strategy . . .
> The challenge for HR is to look at all the areas that they
> encompass and make sure they are integated into the main plan.

But he admitted:

> One of the problems this company used to have up to a few
> years ago was that HR strategy was seen as something com-
> pletely separate from the corporate strategy. What we have
> tried to do, in the past few years is to make them one and the
> same thing.

The Director of Personnel of ABC Distribution recognised that:

> The development of HR strategies should be shared more
> widely with the business controllers. If we don't do that we

114

run the risk of not developing the consistent themes we need to have.

But the Director of Finance was positive that:

> In terms of performance improvement the business and HR strategies are very closely linked. Productivity is a major area and the HR implications of pursuing these policies is critical.

Another positive comment from a Finance Director (Bookworld) was:

> I think more and more we should recognise that there are HR issues in almost everything we do . . . Everything that happens in the company is to do with people and therefore it's almost inconceivable that HR shouldn't be involved with everything.

These, incidentally, were not the only positive contributions from finance directors. We found that, without exception, the eight finance directors we interviewed were all fully aware of the significance of the HR perspective for their organisations, although they were obviously concerned with financial performance and budgets. We may have been fortunate in the finance directors we met – as one personnel director told us: 'Our financial guy is someone who says yes, not like the ones I've met in other organisations.' But our meetings gave the lie to the stereotyped view of accountants as 'number crunchers', or even 'bean counters'. And, at least in these organisations, no support was provided for Peter Armstrong's (1989) contention that 'today's personnel function operates within a managerial culture which is increasingly dominated by the language and structure of management accountancy'.

In Loamshire Council, the approach to integration as described by the Director of Personnel was simply to get the top team together and ask them: 'What are the real strategies that will help the organisation and its functioning?' And the Director of Planning for the authority commented on the important integrating role of the Director of Personnel as follows:

In the old days, the Personnel Manager was not a member of
the management team, and I got used to a culture where personnel advice was not really part of strategic direction. And
any debate there may have been at the corporate level came
out in the wash. It was not led by someone like our Director of
Personnel. She is now on a par with the rest of us in terms of
status and contribution and she brings the whole of the HR
angle into the debate.

And in reply to the question: 'How well are corporate and HR
strategies integrated?' the Director of Technical Services said:

The short answer is that they are inextricably linked . . . You
cannot do anything without having worked through the HR
implications and it's all about better performance by teams
and individuals.

The approach of Megastores was described by the Director of
Stores as follows:

The starting point is the operating plan emerging from and
contributing to the business plan. There is only a certain level
of change we can cope with and what we have is a funnel of
brilliant ideas and strategies, but they all end up in the stores.
So we only commit to a plan we can deliver and we identify
the levels of change that we can manage and calculate how
much time the stores have to implement it. That is fed into the
planning process so that it becomes realistic. The HR strategy
is integral to the process, it's not linked.

The Director of Central Marketing at Megastores also commented
that:

The business and HR strategies are very linked but what I
would say is that whilst the HR support is really quite considerable, it is the business strategy which drives the HR strategy
and not the other way around . . . the business and HR strategies are developed in parallel but at different levels – as are
the marketing and merchandising strategies, the IT strategy
and all the other various strategies that need to be developed
both in terms of implications and in terms of strategy to support the overall business one.

At Pilkington Optronics this is not an issue. As explained by Gordon McLean, Marketing Director:

> We do not think of ourselves as having an HR strategy *per se*. We just see it as one aspect of the overall business strategy. From what I have observed going on in the business I find it quite difficult to separate a strand of activity which I would call HR strategy because it is so integral to everything which is going on . . . HR strategy is effectively a part of the overall vision.

He believes that the level of cultural change encountered over the last few years has necessitated an HR strategy as an integrated part of the business plan: 'It [the HR strategy] was clearly established in the planning process and it had hard objectives in the same way as the business strategy.' He gave the example of the Technical Director who is developing technical route maps, and the personnel function which is working with technical management to produce forecasts as a basis for finding and developing the right people with the right skills. His own role is to explain the nature of the competences required in the business groups, including business management, programme management and sales and marketing: 'Only by understanding these can we equip ourselves for the future.'

At Rover Group, the mission for the company as being 'internationally renowned for extraordinary customer satisfaction' is the integrating theme which unifies all aspects of strategy, including the people strategies. John Towers, Chief Executive said:

> The whole question of the contribution of people to our business has been so open in terms of our strategies and enabling processes over the last few years that probably a large part of our population would suggest that people strategies have actually led processes at the very front end of our thinking, whether it is explicit or implicit . . . We have a company culture which requires everyone when formulating their strategies to recognise the implications for individuals and their job security in whatever they are planning to do.

The Director of Finance for Morton Healthcare Trust said:

> I don't see our personnel strategies as being separate [from
> our corporate strategies]. They [the personnel strategies]
> impact on everything and are fully integrated.

At Motorola the key business strategies of delivering product
quality and customer satisfaction consistent with maintaining an
accepted level of costs are also the drivers for all aspects of functional strategies, including HR. The HR Director totally rejected
the suggestion that at Motorola HR strategies might be downstream
from business (marketing and financial) strategies:

> If there are any HR issues, decisions won't be made without
> the involvement of the HR people, whether it is at corporate
> level or at operational level.

At Albion Bank the business strategies have resulted in a massive
change programme and it was recognised from the outset that HR
strategies were going to be catalysts for that change.

The integration of HR strategies with human and business needs
was emphasised by the Managing Director of Welland Water:

> We keep very close to our people in understanding their hopes
> and aspirations for the future and we seek to maximise the
> match between what they want to do and what the business
> needs.

The Director of Finance for Welland Water pointed out: 'The HR
side is a fundamental part of the business planning process, and it's
not something you just bolt on somewhere along the way.' He also
commented:

> There's a lot of interaction, prior to and during the top board
> discussion which tends to be concerned with culturally based
> issues and the way we manage people.

On the basis of these comments and other observations made by the
directors we interviewed, integration is most likely to be achieved
when:

- there are well-articulated corporate or business strategies operating in the context of a clear mission
- there is a powerful driving force in the shape of commitment to certain values and overall strategies for change
- the chief executive or managing director recognises the contribution that people make to increasing added value and achieving competitive advantage and ensures that people issues are fully taken into account *at the time corporate or business strategies are being prepared*
- the other members of the top team generally share the views of their chief executive on the added value that can be created by considering HR and corporate/business issues simultaneously
- the personnel director is capable of making a full contribution to the formulation of corporate/business strategies as well as those relating to people
- the views of the personnel director are listened to and acted upon

Achieving coherence

The impression we gained from each of the organisations we visited was that there was a strong impetus towards the development and implementation of coherent personnel policies and practices. Frequently, the driving forces behind this thrust for coherence were the overarching strategies or values of the organisation to which everything that was done was related in some way. These could consist of the need for high-quality employees (a general requirement but given particular emphasis in Pilkington Optronics), team working (Motorola), performance improvement (ABC Distribution, Megastores), empowerment (Loamshire Council), quality (Rover Group), flexibility (Morton Healthcare Trust), or values concerning participation (Welland Water). These provided frameworks or points of reference for the development of interrelated programmes which may include the use of competence analysis, performance management, reward and management development processes as the means for achieving coherence.

The impact of strategic HRM

The problem of measuring the impact of strategic HRM on the
bottom line is that the many factors which affect organisational performance make it difficult to isolate the impact of one from the
other. Purcell (1989) has suggested:

> If it were possible to demonstrate that enlightened or progres-
> sive approaches to the management of people were invariably
> associated with higher productivity, lower unit costs and
> improved profit, life would be easier for the HR planner. As it
> is, little can be proved because of the complexity of the vari-
> ables and the impossibility of monitoring and measuring all
> the relevant dynamics and relationships.

It is undoubtedly the case that the variables are complex and that it
is difficult to isolate the different factors contributing to success.
But it can be argued that the highest common factor will be the
contribution of people as individuals or in teams, whether this contribution is to do with strategic management, operational management, professional services or the direct inputs made by employees
to achieving end-results.

Futhermore, if it is accepted that HRM is 'owned and driven' by
line management as an overall approach to the process of managing
people, then it is reasonable to believe that HR strategies will make
a significant impact on results in organisations which do adopt that
approach.

One common ratio that is used to measure this impact is added
value per pound of employment costs. And in these terms, two of
the companies we visited with a strongly strategic approach to
people management have done well in recent years. At Pilkington
Optronics the ratio more than doubled between 1989/90 and
1992/3, and at the Rover Group it improved by 29 per cent between
1991 and 1993. Although in both these cases some of the improvement could be attributed to downsizing, this was part of the HR
strategy, which had to be managed mainly by the HR function.

Views on impact

The following views on the impact of HR strategies were made by different executives:

> Our customers don't want to know what is going on here. All they want to know is that their products are going to be there at the back door of their stores when they wanted them and in the quantities they wanted. So our priority in HR was to make sure that our employees were able to meet that challenge. (Director of Personnel, ABC Distribution)

> I see the added-value contribution in terms of flexibility, a willingness to tackle the new and the different, and underlying security in so doing. (Director of Finance, ABC Distribution)

> Over a period of time HR has had quite a lot of impact but it's not measurable . . . It has, however, contributed to the stability of the business by building up long-term relationships with the workforce and trade unions. And the quality initiative, in which the HR side played a very significant role, will make a major difference to the business. (Director of Network Business, ABC Distribution)

> I think it's genuinely difficult to assess the impact of HR policies and practices because they are there and you can't test what would happen if they weren't there. One could only say that certain things wouldn't be done; there would be a deterioration in the training and ability of people and a deterioration in their ability to meet objectives because there would not be the framework to measure these things. We've never questioned the need for an HR department. It's rather like a building; it would be hard to run the business out in the street. (Chief Executive, Bookworld)

> We cannot measure the impact of our HR strategies on profitability. Elsewhere, in our development centres for example, we are forever seeking the answer to measuring impact, but it is a very difficult thing to do. The measurement has not progressed beyond the response, the verbal response, the feedback from the people who have been on the sessions, and the feedback from Board members on what has happened and what benefits they are seeing in the broadening of

the individual . . . But there is total support for what I do from the Board, and that's ongoing. Therefore, immeasurable though it may be, it is a sign of acceptance that we are contributing. (HR Director, Bookworld)

We would be a lot poorer without HR but we couldn't measure how much poorer we would be. (HR Director, Bookworld)

The difference we've made is about freeing up the organisation, releasing initiative and empowering people. I think it is the whole strategy of empowerment that changed the culture of the organisation, and that's what pleases me more than anything. (Director of Personnel, Loamshire Council)

I think that the work that has been done in devolving some of the personnel management issues from the centre has made a significant contribution because the issue of managing people is put fairly and squarely where it belongs. It does not belong at the centre with people who are not involved on a day-to-day basis with the people actually delivering the service. The management of people in all its glory lies with the managers who are using their people as front-line deliverers and I think that has been an important strategy for us and one that the Director of Personnel managed very successfully and I think has been a significant contribution to all these issues about human resourcing; it has gone very well. (Director of Community Services, Loamshire Council)

I don't think we have any evidence in a scientific sense that the philosophy and style of the Trust produces a better outcome than, say, an autocratic style which would represent a diametrically opposite approach. We are running the Trust on the basis of some hypotheses and these hypotheses remain to be tested. On the other hand, there are a number of things we can point to. The amount of change that has taken place within the Trust is a result of placing the responsibility in the hands of people doing the work. Had it been imposed from above as an edict there would have been more strife and much less would have been achieved. I think that people's ownership of what they are doing is crucial and they are flexible to a degree that did not exist five years ago. People who, five years ago, might have been devoted to defending their own corner, are now much more interested in co-operating to achieve the work of their sub-directorate. (Medical Director, Morton Healthcare Trust)

The added value we get is that we have had a pretty decent supply of well-trained managers to sustain our business growth. (Managing Director, Megastores)

There are a number of measures in which Megastores are very favourable. Whether or not it's a result of the HR strategy or a result of the business strategy together with a complementary HR strategy I'm not sure but our staff retention is very good and staff turnover very low. We seem to be able to attract and retain some pretty good people. (Director of Central Marketing, Megastores)

The following sequence of questions and the answers given to them by the Director of Personnel for Megastores provide some insight into what HR can contribute and how that contribution can be measured:

Q. What overall impact do you think your HR strategies have had on the performance of your organisation in terms of added value?

A. Very significant: performance management, competence frameworks, work-based learning (which we've got great expertise in) and going through the IIP process all contribute to making us see how important people are within the organisation.

Q. What evidence do you have that your HR strategies have made a real contribution?

A. Pretty easy to answer. Look at the performance of the company, which is only really as good as the people in it. Our performance as a retailer has been well above par in one of the hardest recessions. We measure the things we introduce and then say, 'Let's take those that have had a substantial and measurable effect', although there are some bits of the HR strategy that have contributed zilch or we can't prove what they have contributed. At the end of the day, however, you can't take HR or sales, marketing or finance and say that it's all down to HR or to good finance or good marketing. It's about how a company operates overall and the HR strategy has got to work within all the other function links to make the business tick.

Q. How do you measure the impact of your HR policies?

A. We can measure a lot. We look at the major projects and
    investments in people in exactly the same way as we
    would look at any other capital investment in the com-
    pany. I need to be able to argue my corner in executive
    meetings that if we put on a training programme there
    will be a gain in sales or efficiency . . . So we subject our-
    selves to the same rigorous financial investment disci-
    plines as other functions have to do.

John Towers believed that Rover Group's emphasis on people
development to improve their contribution to the business was a
major factor in achieving competitive advantage, and there was
general agreement amongst the other Rover Group line directors
whom we interviewed that this was the case.

This approach to assessing the impact of HR policies is in line
with what Geoff Armstrong, Director General of The Institute of
Personnel and Development said to us on this subject:

> You measure the impact by measuring the ability of the organ-
> isation to adapt and flex and meet customer needs faster than
> its competitors.

But apart from general added-value figures such as those mentioned above, no one could point to a specific contribution of
strategic HRM to the bottom line which could be measured in
financial terms. There was simply a general, largely subjective,
belief that, alongside other strategic initiatives, an integrated
approach to strategic HRM did pay off.

The problem of tangibility, especially in financial terms, kept on
cropping up. The Chief Executive of Morton Healthcare Trust, for
example, thought that 'the real evidences are quite intangible'. And
the Managing Director of Welland Water remarked:

> I don't think you can point to pounds and pence and say it's has
> this effect. It's virtually impossible to say that there's been an
> improvement in performance, an improvement on the bottom
> line, and that this is attributable to our HR values; and I find it
> very difficult to imagine how you can positively measure it . . .
> Your real measure is just talking to people. It's very difficult to
> persuade accountants of that and I am an accountant.

However, the Head of Personnel of Welland Water did believe that 'our HR strategies have created an environment in which people can do well'.

Our research led us to the conclusion that there is no point in seeking some magic formula which will provide a convincing answer on exactly what impact the HR strategies of an organisation have made on the bottom line. It is possible to point to specific areas where performance has been improved as a result of HR initiatives and attempts can and should be made to assess the added-value contribution of such initiatives. But a final and definitive answer on the overall impact in financial terms is unlikely to emerge, and it is probably pointless to look for one. All that can be done is to say in effect:

- Our organisation is successful in measurable terms and this has been achieved by the efforts of our people.
- Our organisation has well-developed and effective HR strategies which are fully integrated with corporate or business strategies and are owned and delivered by line management.
- Therefore, our HR strategies have made a significant contribution to the success of the organisation.

And that is the essence of the argument presented by a number of the directors we interviewed. As one finance director replied to a question about the overall impact of their HR strategies, 'Well, they must have had a major impact given that we are so successful.'

The evidence from other research

The evidence from other research concerning the impact of strategic HRM on performance is neither consistent nor conclusive.

Research conducted by David Guest and Kim Hogue (1994) has indeed provided evidence that organisations with HR strategies formally endorsed and actively supported by top management are better at weathering the recession and are more successful in terms of quality, productivity, absenteeism levels and labour turnover levels. The analysis, based on responses from personnel directors or line managers in more than 120 non-union greenfield sites, revealed differences in company performance, depending on the kind of HR strategy employed. For example, those respondents who were identified as having clear and wide-ranging HRM policies reported labour turnover of 7 per cent during 1992 compared with 14 per cent among those who did not have a planned HR strategy. Absenteeism rates showed a similar pattern. The strong establishments in HRM policy terms tended to be British- rather than American-owned, and were often part of a larger organisation. German-owned sites were most likely to report a low take-up of HRM techniques. According to this research, the strong HR sites were more likely to have the commitment of lower-grade staff and to have line-management support for their HRM policies and practices. Little difference was found in the use of HR policies and practices between union and non-union sites.

An alternative view was expressed by Brewster (1993) on the basis of his analysis of HRM in Europe. He concluded that, while it is frequently argued that firms which adopt a strategic HRM approach will perform better, the evidence at the national level points in the opposite direction: 'Countries with less evidence of HRM . . . tend to have been most successful in recent years.'

And Richard Whipp (1992) has poured cold water on the belief that the introduction of strategic HRM is guaranteed to improve performance:

> The hope that HRM can be easily linked to the competitive performance of a firm is illusory. In the UK at least there is a real danger that the HRM label is being applied to firms inaccurately. In practice, the disarray of the competitive process is mirrored by the fragility and impermanence of many HRM instruments.

In a sense, he is right. Strategic HRM by itself cannot guarantee improved performance. There are so many other factors involved. But an integrated approach to HRM which focuses on the key levers for performance improvements as identified by management and which develops mutually supportive programmes for this purpose can make a major contribution, and this was demonstrated by our research. This is most likely to be the case when performance improvements are achieved by concentrating on particular 'drivers' such as total quality, continuous improvement, performance management or team working.

The impact of strategic HRM on performance will inevitably be a function of a number of interdependent factors, but the role of the HR function, as discussed in the third part of this book, is crucial.

What are the most characteristic features of strategic HRM in action?

To summarise, the most characteristic features of strategic HRM in action in the case-study companies were:

- A clear and purposeful corporate or business strategy exists.
- The HR strategies in most cases are fully integrated and owned by the whole of the top management team.
- The HR strategies are very much concerned with developing the organisation and the people in it.
- Most if not all of the organisations we visited could be described as 'unitarist' in their approach (ie they believe in the commonality of the interests of management and employees), and they are all striving to develop a 'commitment-orientated' culture. But in many cases, as described in Chapter 5, they have still taken pains to involve the trade unions in their change strategies on a partnership basis.
- HR strategies relate to the critical success factors of the organisation and the impact high-quality and committed people can make on the delivery of the results the organisation is expected to achieve.

Overall conclusions on strategic HRM in action

Our analysis of the content of HR strategy in the organisations we
studied is that it is largely concerned with overall issues related to
the values and culture of the organisation and its people-manage-
ment philosophies, organisational performance, individual competence, quality, participation, empowerment and flexibility. Matching
the quality of people available to the requirements of the organisation
was another important issue.

Assessing the characteristics of these organisations against the
criteria listed at the end of Chapter 3 leads to the following conclusions:

1. The top management of each organisation could be
   described as adopting a strategic management approach
   although, naturally, how they did this varied considerably.
2. There was a process for developing corporate/business
   strategies in each organisation but the degree to which this
   was formalised varied widely.
3. The corporate/business strategies clearly expressed the
   intentions of top management, although not necessarily in
   a highly formalised way.
4. Top management in these organisations seemed on the
   whole to be adopting what could very broadly be described
   as a strategic HRM approach in that they were aware of the
   importance of giving careful consideration to the strategic
   personnel issues alongside their corporate/business strategy
   concerns (although none of them referred to what they
   were doing as 'strategic HRM').
5. This approach did result in the development of HR strategies which addressed the key longer-term people issues of
   the organisations and clearly expressed the intentions of
   top management.
6. The HR strategies seem on the whole to be well integrated
   with the corporate/business strategies.
7. There appeared to be a fair degree of coherence in the personnel policies and programmes developed as a result of
   these strategies.
8. The approaches adopted in these organisations broadly
   conform to the meanings of strategic HRM as defined by
   Hendry and Pettigrew (1986), ie planning, coherence,

matching HR strategy to an explicit business strategy and treating people as a strategic resource.

9. The organisations do generally appear to be pursuing David Guest's (1989b) four policy goals, ie:

- **strategic integration**. Personnel and business strategies are integrated and across policy areas it appears that HR practices are accepted and used by line managers as part of their everyday work.
- **high commitment.** The management teams in these organisations appear to be concerned with achieving 'behavioural commitment' in the sense of pursuing agreed goals and 'attitudinal commitment' to develop strong identification amongst all employees with the enterprise.
- **high quality.** Although TQM is not operated as a package in any of the organisations we visited, the philosophy of TQM does appear to have influenced management thinking and approach, sometimes very strongly, as at Rover Group. In these organisations, in David Guest's (1989b) words, a policy of 'investment in high quality employees' existed which in turn bears directly on the quality of the products or services delivered.
- **flexibility**. There is much concern about the achievement of flexibility both in terms of organisation structures (there is often a strong focus on teamwork) and individual roles. For example, the emphasis on 'process' at Rover, which to a remarkable degree was shared by all the members of the top team we saw, is essentially a strategy for flexibility.

10. So far as we can judge, the strategies adopted by these organisations have provided effective guidelines for decision-making, have been acted on and have made a significant impact on organisational performance, although it is difficult if not impossible to measure this in financial terms.

In considering HR strategies, however, there are two points which should be emphasised. The first is that strategies are only meaningful if they are turned into effective action. The second is that, having turned strategies into action programmes, steps have to

be taken to ensure that people (individuals and teams) are accountable for making them work. Lawrie Rumens, General Manager at
Pilkington Optronics expressed this point well:

> There must be a strong emphasis on accountability. If you are
> not in control, if you are not well planned and co-ordinated, if
> you don't have the disciplines to make it happen and be prof-
> itable, then you haven't got anything. And I believe that if you
> can't measure it you can't control it, and if you don't control it
> you won't achieve success.

Part Three:

The Contribution of the HR Function

7

The Roles of the Personnel Director and the Personnel Function

Research findings

In the organisations we visited there seemed to be general agreement amongst all the chief executives and directors we met that the role of the personnel director was to be very much part of the top team, sharing responsibility with his or her colleagues for the success of the organisation. In some organisations the role was more that of supporting the achievement of the corporate strategy; in others, the personnel director was expected to make a full contribution as, in effect, a business partner.

There was a marked tendency in a number of the organisations, such as Pilkington Optronics, Rover Group and Loamshire Council to 'empower' line managers to deal with their own personnel concerns. As the Director of Personnel of Loamshire Council, 'We are keen to encourage directors to develop their expertise in HR management, not just at operational level, but also at strategic level.'

A selection of the views expressed to us is set out below.

Views of chief executives and other directors

> What I want and what I get is a general contribution: whether the individual is HR Director, Finance Director or Marketing Director is in many ways irrelevant. (Managing Director, ABC Distribution)

> I look at the HR Director in the same way as the Finance Director, which is that when we are talking about business policy and business strategy they would play into that at a general level and, having sorted out the policy, they contribute in their specific areas. (Managing Director, ABC Distribution)

> The role of HR is to facilitate whatever we are trying to do. (Deputy Managing Director, ABC Distribution)

133

I would expect him [the Director of Personnel] to be visionary, to see a bigger picture than I can see and to be able to articulate that. There is an element of added value in balancing HR policies with business issues. (Director of Finance, ABC Distribution)

I would expect two levels of contribution from the HR director. Firstly he should contribute to the business process as a member of the collective team. Secondly, he clearly has another level of input which is as a pure HR specialist. In that respect I would see him contributing on infrastructure issues relating to strategy such as management succession, talent development, and on specific issues such as those relating to acquisitions. (Director of Finance, ABC Distribution)

The Director of Personnel and I have shared vision about the role of organisations and how they should function, and a shared vision of personnel and HR management, so I get what I want and it is delivered very effectively. (Chief Executive, Loamshire Council)

One of the roles of HR is to create an environment in which line managers think it right to build plans for people and carry out appraisals. The personnel function also has responsibility for organisation and management structure and that is a very important role that they play. (Managing Director, Megastores)

Our strategic plans are debated at executive 'away days' and each director, irrespective of whether they have functional responsibility for an initiative whatever it may be, is encouraged to contribute their views – so that in essence the strategic plans have common ownership. As a member of the executive [committee], the Director of Personnel would be encouraged and expected to chip in irrespective of whether it was a personnel issue or a distribution issue or a merchandise issue or a store format issue. (Director of Central Marketing, Megastores)

Our Personnel Director is the champion of the idea that nothing gets done other than when it is done by people. (Director of Stores, Megastores)

We see the Health Service as heavily a personnel organisation. It's much more important to have a personnel director than a marketing director or a commercial director. (Chief Executive, Morton Healthcare Trust)

The need for rapid change at the strategic level means taking the workforce with you. So the function is more intimately involved in strategic planning within the company than we might previously have anticipated, because of the need to communicate and facilitate changes in culture and working practices. We could not do without that support. (Marketing Director, Pilkington Optronics)

Any member of the top team, irrespective of whether they are in personnel or engineering, should be spending a considerable amount of time thinking strategically and really stretching the boundaries of what we believe ourselves to be capable of doing. (Chief Executive, Rover Group)

Members of the personnel function act as agents of change rather than changers, and the improvements occurring within the organisation can only occur as a result of well-motivated and skilled personnel people operating in conjunction with well-motivated and skilled management people. (Chief Executive, Rover Group)

The role of the Personnel Director is to make sure that all of the people aspects are placed firmly on the table when we are making business decisions and not left on one side as we used to. (Managing Director, Product Supply, Rover Group)

The essential role of the HR function is to create an environment in which everyone has the freedom and confidence to maximise their contribution. (Managing Director, Welland Water)

The Head of Personnel creates a framework that the line managers subscribe to and perceive as relevant to what they want, and then their commitment to implement it is total. (Managing Director, Welland Water)

Views of personnel directors

We found that what is sometimes referred to as the 'business manager' model was characteristic of the views of the personnel directors we met, as the following quotations show:

> We have spearheaded the development of processes for internal marketing. Our whole HR strategy has been consumer focused and based on a consultancy and commercial model. (Director of Personnel, Loamshire Council)

> Basically, I have agreed with my team that we will be business partners in each business; we will have the understanding of what is going on to converse knowledgeably with any of the business people. (HR Director, Motorola)

> First and foremost I am a director of the company. The fact that I happen to be head of personnel is secondary. So while I am basically at the table as the head of personnel I have to be able to contribute on all aspects of the business. Certainly more than half my time is spent dealing with business opportunities and business problems, not necessarily people problems, and as a businessman rather than a leading light in personnel. So my role in the main is as a generalist, but if there are any people aspects to be looked at then obviously I would be the one to be in the lead, but from the point of view of the overall business. (Personnel Director, Pilkington Optronics)

> The role that I play in the company is essentially to develop people strategies which are the most appropriate for achieving our business objectives . . . It carries with it enough freedom to make recommendations and proposals about the best way we should operate to achieve those objectives. (Personnel Director, Rover Group)

Other views on the role

Over the years the personnel function has come in for a lot of criticism. It started with Peter Drucker's (1955) rhetorical question: 'Is personnel management bankrupt?' (on the whole he thought not), and it has gone on ever since, culminating in the London School of Economics report (Fernie, Metcalf and Woodland, 1994) which, on the basis of impeccable statistical analysis built on a foundation of sand in the shape of subjective opinions about 'climate', came to the conclusion that 'having a personnel specialist in the workplace and/or a director responsible for HRM on the board is no guarantee of good relations'.

David Guest's contribution

A more balanced contribution to the debate was made by David Guest (1991) on the basis of research, also conducted by the London School of Economics, on perceptions of the influence and effectiveness of personnel managers among line managers and personnel specialists. This revealed that:

1. Personnel and line managers choose a wide range of criteria to judge personnel management effectiveness.
2. A consistent set of topics are rated more or less effective and there is a reasonable consensus in this respect between line and personnel managers:
   - effectiveness is high in the administration area of people processing and in the high-profile areas of industrial relations and employment legislation
   - effectiveness is low in the more proactive areas such as employee motivation and involvement.
3. Both line managers and personnel managers accept that personnel managers have little influence and should have more.
4. Line managers' ratings of personnel management effectiveness are consistently lower than the ratings given by personnel managers themselves – line managers felt that problems in achieving effectiveness were particularly severe among personnel people.

However, Guest notes: 'One of the consistent outcomes of research on personnel management is that personnel managers are less effective than they should be.'

The Young Samuel Chambers research

The Young Samuel Chambers unpublished 1992 research for the
Personnel Standards Lead Body (PSLB) also revealed some important dilemmas for organisations which created problems for personnel specialists, namely:

- both devolving power lower down the organisation and aligning
  the activities of these units through a central strategic thrust
- both managing growth and having smaller units
- both encouraging innovation and risk and reinforcing efficiency
  and standardisation
- both being commercial and market orientated and recognising
  public responsibilities
- both encouraging change and adaptation and ensuring stability
  and predictability
- both having universal or international standards and having particular or local responsiveness

The Young Samuel Chambers report referred to the 'old style personnel practitioner' who was mainly concerned with specialist
tools and understanding organisations and human behaviour. They
noted that many of the chief executives they spoke to expressed
strong views about the limitations of this approach. These included:

- an excessive concern with rules and procedures that amounted
  sometimes to policing and blocking action
- a tendency to introduce systems and procedures that were not
  appropriate to the business context and not owned by line management, which therefore failed
- an indiscriminate approach to being a 'good employer' so that
  the company was, to quote from one respondent, 'drowned in
  goodness'

But they contrasted this type of approach with people in personnel who were more orientated to business management, consultant processes and people and organisations, and not so concerned

with the specialist tools aspects of their work. This approach was identified as important in today's conditions because:

- chief executives need a person near to them who can 'read' the organisation, its political nuances and the particular personal complexities of those near the top whose behaviour can have such a marked impact on business performance – many want honest feedback, even confrontation if necessary
- the recognition that implementation and even strategising itself has to come from all parts of the organisation, not just the top, creates a much greater need for process skills
- in many organisations, the devolution of control to units means that influence can only be achieved through means more akin to consultant behaviour

The Personnel Standards Lead Body Functional Survey

The PSLB's (1994) functional survey revealed that:

- Line management and personnel tend to be equally involved in areas of strategy and organisation, resourcing and performance enhancement. Personnel tend to be more involved than line management when dealing in the areas of compensation and benefits and in some of the key areas of relationships with employees.
- The personnel function demonstrates most competence in the areas of recruitment, pay and benefits administration as well as in promoting joint consultation and procedures for handling grievances and discipline.
- The areas perceived to be of high importance to organisational success and where the personnel function demonstrated *least* competence were in effective communication, performance management, enhancing individual capability, long-term individual and team development, internal movement of employees and identifying individual potential.
- No real differences were found in the ratings of importance or competence between public- and private-sector, single- or multiple-site and large or small organisations.

Models of personnel management

We found that there was quite a degree of similarity in the roles played by the personnel directors of the organisations we visited in that, as members of the top team, they were involved in both corporate and HR strategic issues and were considered to be playing a valuable corporate role which went far beyond the provision of effective personnel services, although it was important that this did take place.

But it would be wrong to assume from this tiny sample that the same situation exists to any large extent elsewhere. There is, of course, an immense diversity in personnel roles which is directly related to the immense diversity in organisations and in the people who run them. It is not possible to say that there is such a thing as a universal prescription for strategic HRM – it will exist in all sorts of forms if it exists at all. Nor is it possible to say that there is one universal model for personnel management. A number of different models have been suggested, and these are described below.

The Karen Legge models

Karen Legge (1978) distinguishes between two models of personnel managers:

1. **conformist innovators**, who go along with their organisation's ends and adjust their means to achieve them. Their expertise is used as a source of professional power to improve the position of their departments
2. **deviant innovators**, who attempt to change this means/ends relationship by gaining acceptance for a different set of criteria for the evaluation of organisational success and their contribution to it

The Shaun Tyson models

These models were established by Tyson (1985) following research which identified three approaches to personnel management in the United Kingdom:

1. **the administrative/support model**, in which personnel officers concentrate on the basics of a routine activity
2. **the systems/reactive model**, which exists in more sophisticated industrial relations environments where the main sphere of influence is on the creation and maintenance of the rules of the work, through policies and procedures
3. **the business manager model**, where the main characteristics of the personnel specialists are that they:
   - integrate their activities closely with top management and ensure that they serve a long-term strategic purpose
   - have the capacity to spot business opportunities, to see the broad picture and to see how their personnel role can help to achieve the company's business ends

The Shaun Tyson/Alan Fell models

Perhaps the best-known models are those developed by Tyson and Fell (1986). These were derived from the former's initial (1985) version. Tyson and Fell's three personnel management models are:

1. **the clerk of works model**. In this model all authority for action is vested in line managers. Personnel policies are formed or created after the actions which created the need. Policies are not integral to the business and are short-term and *ad hoc*. Authority is vested in line managers and personnel activities are largely routine – employment and day-to-day administration.
2. **the contracts manager model**. In this model policies are well established, often implicit, with a heavy industrial relations emphasis, possibly derived from an employers' association. The personnel department will use fairly sophisticated systems, especially in the field of employee relations. The personnel manager is likely to be a professional or very experienced in industrial relations. He or she will not be on the Board and, although having some authority to police the implementation of policies, acts mainly in an interpretive, not a creative or innovative role.

3. **the architect model**. In this model explicit personnel policies exist as part of the corporate strategy. HR planning and development are important concepts and a long-term view is taken. Systems tend to be sophisticated. The head of the personnel function is probably on the Board and his or her power is derived from professionalism and a perceived contribution to the business.

The 'contractor' model is probably less common now since the relative decline of the importance of the industrial relations aspects of the personnel manager's work.

The Kathleen Monks models

Kathleen Monks' (1992) survey of personnel practices in 97 organisations in Ireland identified four models which extend the Legge/Tyson and Fell concepts:

1. **traditional/administrative**. This applied to about one-third of the organisations. The personnel department in this model is very much a support function with a focus on administrative matters, record keeping and adherence to rules and regulations. Few initiatives were taken by these personnel departments.
2. **traditional/industrial relations**. These organisations (20 of the sample) concentrated on industrial relations and had elaborate manuals and procedures to deal with industrial relations matters. But other personnel matters such as recruitment and selection were not given a high priority. Personnel managers could meet company expectations if they 'kept the show on the road'. This model corresponds broadly to Tyson and Fell's (1986) 'contracts manager'.
3. **innovative/professional**. Thirty-five organisations were defined as 'innovative/professional'. The approach of the personnel specialists in these firms was professional and expert. They were concerned to dismantle the problematic elements of traditional practices with the expectation that whatever emerged had to be better than the existing system. Their firms had well-established

activities in such areas as manpower planning, remuneration, training and development, with computerised record systems.
4. **innovative/sophisticated**. In these mainly high-tech or finance-sector organisations (only nine out of the 97, eight of which were foreign-owned) personnel issues were integrated into strategic plans, personnel was represented on the Board and was recognised as an important function within the organisation. Commitment was sought by the intensive use of recruitment and selection practices involving a wide range of tests and several interviews to get the 'right' type of people. The manufacturing firms in this category had implemented programmes such as multi-skilling and job rotation and there was some use of autonomous work groups. Investment in employees involved spending a lot of money on training.

The John Storey model

Storey's (1992a) model suggests a two-dimensional map: interventionary/non-interventionary and strategic/tactical. From this he identified four roles:

1. **change makers** (interventionary/strategic), which is close to the HRM model
2. **advisors** (non-interventionary/strategic), who act as internal consultants, leaving much of HR practice to the line managers
3. **regulators** (interventionary/tactical), who are 'managers of discontent' concerned with formulating and monitoring employment rules
4. **handmaidens** (non-interventionary/tactical), who merely provide a service to meet the demands of line managers

The role model for strategic HRM

The role model for personnel involvement in a strategic HRM context corresponds broadly with the:

- deviant innovator role (Legge)

- business manager role (Tyson)
- architect role (Tyson and Fell)
- innovative/sophisticated role (Monks)
- change makers role (Storey)

The reality of strategic HRM is probably that if personnel directors with the support of their staff are not capable of adopting these sorts of roles, or are working in an environment which is unreceptive to the principles of HRM, the extent to which they can make a strategic contribution will be small. In the former case strategic HRM will function without them – they will have 'given it away'. In the latter case, strategic HRM is unlikely to happen unless there is a change of heart at the top and/or, importantly, the personnel director has the capacity and will-power either to exploit or to encourage the change.

The capabilities required of HR directors in order to play a useful and necessary part in an organisation practising strategic HRM and the approaches they can adopt are discussed below.

Capabilities required of HR directors and personnel professionals

On the basis of their research, the PSLB (1993) stated that to be respected members of the top management team senior personnel professionals must:

- demonstrate to all their colleagues a real contribution to business processes, customer requirements, general management and the operation of the business
- 'read the organisation' for the chief executive and provide assistance in developing team and individual performance among the top group to achieve corporate objectives
- exercise judgement in supporting or opposing executive actions – providing a balancing or opposing force when the actions may be cost-effective in the short term but damaging to morale or

productivity at the time or in the longer term.

Their functional survey (1994) reported that one of the main changes their respondents believed was necessary in the personnel function was 'the need to demonstrate an increased contribution to business performance'.

The importance of the 'business partner' role was underlined by Coulson-Thomas's (1991) research which indicated that a personnel director:

> . . . needs to have a thorough understanding of the finances of the company and to be able to speak with authority on the company's business performance.

The future role

IBM and Towers Perrin in their report *Priorities for Competitive Advantage* (1992) suggested that in the year 2000, human resource management will be:

- responsive to a highly competitive market place and global business structures
- closely linked to business plans
- jointly conceived and implemented by line and HR managers
- focused on quality, customer service, productivity, employee involvement, teamwork, and workplace flexibility.

The report comments:

> Human resources is being transformed from a specialised, stand-alone function to a broad corporate competency in which HR and line managers build partnerships to gain competitive advantage and achieve overall business goals.

Other current research sponsored by the Institute of Personnel and Development is also establishing an increasing tendency for line managers to take the responsibility for HR, with the personnel function having more of an internal consultancy role although it might continue to provide administrative services.

The findings relating to the UK and Ireland contained in the data collected in a European study conducted by the European Association for Personnel Management and the International Institute for Management Development (Brooklyn Derr et al. 1993) indicated that in future personnel managers must not only continue to deliver impeccable personnel management and organisation development services, but must also be knowledgeable about the firm's central competences, key values, competitive environment and customer demands.

The respondents to this survey rated the most significant forces affecting their profession in the next five years as the need to improve quality and to provide better customer service, changes in organisational structures, technological innovation and the shortage of skilled workers. Organisations of the future will require both strategic and specialist services from their personnel professionals. These findings correspond precisely with what we established from our research.

8

The Contribution Made by the HR Function to Added Value and Competitive Advantage

As Geoff Armstrong, Director General of the Institute of Personnel and Development said to us:

> We are at the time when people are the critical distinguishing feature between organisations. And the effectiveness with which people are trained and developed, motivated and managed is the single most controllable dimension available to managers.

In this chapter we consider the role of the HR function in enhancing this process, thus adding value and achieving competitive advantage.

The creation of added value

In accounting language, added value is the difference between the income of the business arising from sales (output) and the amount spent on materials and other purchased services (input). In more general terms, it is the development and use of any resource in a way which ensures that it yields a substantial and sustainable higher return on whatever has been invested in it. Added value often means the creation of more out of less, and an increasingly popular index of overall organisational performance is added value per pound of employment costs. The term added value is also used more colloquially to indicate anything extra which can be created by the investment of resources, effort or time in the delivery of a desired result. In broad terms it can refer to the difference between inputs and positive outputs.

Added value is created by people. It is people at various levels in the organisations who create visions, define values and missions, set goals, develop strategic plans and implement those plans in accordance with the underpinning values. Added value will be enhanced by anything that is done to obtain and develop the right sort of people, to motivate and manage them effectively, to gain their commitment to organisational values, to build and maintain stable relationships with them, to develop the right sort of organisational structure, and to deploy them effectively and productively in that structure.

An added value approach to HR will be directed positively to improve employee motivation, commitment, skill, performance and contribution. It can aim to get better value for money from HR expenditure in such areas as training, reward and employee benefits. More negatively, it can focus on the reduction of employment costs.

Views of the PSLB

The PSLB (1993) has defined the key purpose of personnel management as being to 'enable people to enhance the individual and collective contributions of people to the short and long term success of the enterprise'. It suggested that to provide value-added contributions personnel professionals must:

- ensure that personnel strategies, policies, operating initiatives and services are aligned to the business needs and priorities
- generate a real ownership of personnel solutions among managers and their people
- manage change – initiating and promoting it when appropriate, providing a stabilising force when change would be damaging
- generate respect when intervening to maintain adherence to personnel policy, balancing short- and long-term issues

Lessons from our research

We asked the people we interviewed how they saw their HR strategies contributing to the creation of added value. We were particularly interested in the opinions of finance directors on the grounds that the latter, at least, should know added value when they see it. But we also obtained the views of other directors.

Chief executives

The following views were expressed by chief executives:

> The tangible contributions made by HR strategies to the success of the business have been providing managers for the business, providing a stable foundation for us to take cost out of the business, and dealing with the integration of people from other companies into our own business. (Managing Director, ABC Distribution)

> Q. What contribution has your Personnel Director made to adding value?
> A. A lot; he has personally generated the NVQ programme, competitive advantage training and training in interpersonal skills. Manpower planning has also been important. (Managing Director, Megastores)

> Personnel have to work with the line managers within technology (which is the driving force of our business) using the best practices and standards within their profession to make sure that we have the required levels of competence. This means planning for five to ten years ahead. Our CIM [computer integrated manufacturing] strategy indicates that within the next ten years we are going to need very different sorts of people in this company. We will need leaders with a technical mainstream knowledge who are also broad enough to cover commercial and other business issues. Personnel has a tremendous role to play in providing that sort of person. (Managing Director, Pilkington Optronics)

> If you look at the rate of improvement we have achieved, you will see that, compared to others, it has been quite significant

... Now there has to be a reason for that somewhere and I think that it is self-evident that you can't get this sort of improvement unless you get individual commitment, unless you achieve that extra 10 per cent from people who are really interested and committed to what they are doing. (Managing Director, Welland Water)

Finance directors

I would see added value in such things as flexibility, a willingness to tackle the new and different and an underlying security in so doing. (Director of Finance, ABC Distribution)

The added value provided by HR is in supporting the business by ensuring the most important resource – its people – is available. (Finance Director, Bookworld)

When we talk about the performance of the authority, one of the things that people want to see is that they are valued. If they believe they are, than a natural consequence will be that the services we provide will be of a higher standard than would otherwise have been the case. (Director of Finance, Loamshire Council)

HR has to provide the means and the wherewithal to help management bring about change . . . The company has been so successful because it is always involved in change. (Finance Director, Megastores)

People are looking after their areas better, and feel that they are contributing more and that they are listened to, and, if you like, that they have been empowered. And because of that we have managed to cope with things that in the past we wouldn't have coped with. (Finance Director, Morton Healthcare Trust)

Q. What impact have your HR strategies and policies had on the performance of the organisation in terms of added value and productivity?
A. Very significant I would say. The HR department has been very fundamentally involved in creating a culture of openness between staff and management, creating a culture of empowerment, so that you don't have to refer everything to your boss to make a decision. I think that

has contributed to significant improvements in productivity, there's no doubt about it. (Finance Director, Welland Water)

Other directors

One of the things I expect our Director of Human Resources to do is to keep the unions quiet, which he does very nicely. I don't mean he keeps them quiet by beating them up. He keeps them quiet by involving them. (Director of Operations, Morton Healthcare Trust)

The policies of openness and support and of being specific about what jobs are going and why, and preparing in advance, have made things go very smoothly. And full marks to our Personnel Director because he has been the leader of these exercises and the creator of these standards and I take my hat off to him. (General Manager, Pilkington Optronics)

The added value comes from using people in the best way, creating an environment that allows them to do the best job possible with a clear objective of what they are trying to achieve for the company. (Director of Operations, Welland Water)

Contribution to achieving and maintaining competitive advantage

Competitive advantage arises out of a firm creating value for its customers, and the ability to gain and retain competitive advantage is crucial to a firm's growth and prosperity.

Unique talents among employees, including superior performance, high productivity, flexibility, innovation and the ability to deliver high levels of personal customer service are ways in which people provide a critical ingredient in developing an organisation's competitive position. People also provide the key to managing the pivotal interdependencies across functional activities and the important external relationships. It can be argued that one of the clear benefits arising from competitive advantage based on the effective management of people is that such an advantage is hard to imitate. An organisation's HRM strategies, policies and practices are a unique blend of procedures, personalities, styles, capabilities and organisational culture.

Achieving competitive advantage

Research conducted recently by the European Association for Personnel Management and the International Institute for Management Development (Brooklyn Derr et al. 1993) revealed that competitive advantage is achieved by developing core competences in the workforce through traditional services (recruitment, reward, career pathing, employee development), and by dealing effectively with macro concerns such as corporate culture, management development and organisational structure.

The IBM/Towers Perrin (1992) world-wide survey of 2,961 firms established that the top five initiatives for gaining competitive advantage as assessed by line managers and HR executives were as in Table 8.1

Table 8.1

	Line	HR
Identify high-potential employees early.	1	4
Communicate directions, plans, problems.	2	1
Reward innovation and creativity.	3	5
Reward customer service and quality.	4	2
Reward business and/or productivity gains.	5	3

Linking competitive and HR strategies

HR strategies can be linked with the three basic competitive strategies as defined by Michael Porter (1985): innovation, quality enhancement and cost reduction (cost leadership).

Linking HRM strategies to foster innovation can involve:

- selecting and developing highly skilled people
- giving them more discretion – using minimal controls
- providing more resources for experimentation
- allowing occasional failure
- appraising performance on the basis of its potential long-term contribution.

An integrated strategy for quality enhancement requires the development of a quality-orientated culture by:

- driving through quality initiatives
- appraising and rewarding people in line with their performance in upholding organisational values for quality and for achieving quality targets
- facilitating the achievement of high quality through recruitment and selection, induction training, continuous improvement programmes, organisation (for example, self-managing teams), and, of course, communicating the need for high quality and the expectations of the organisation about quality performance

The achievement of cost leadership can be supported by:

- taking cost out of the business by developing a leaner, fitter organisation – this will include identifying the scope for reducing headcounts without disrupting key organisational activities, and managing the process in a way which is both humane and minimises disruption
- productivity planning – generally considering any means of increasing productivity in terms of cost per unit of output through reorganisation, training or reward practices and the introduction of new technology
- new technology introduction – helping with the introduction of new technology by identifying the necessary competences, finding and developing the skilled people required, providing training or retraining, getting those affected involved in the development

process and consulting with employees and their union representatives on any employment implications

Methods

How do organisations actually set about maximising added value
and achieving competitive advantage through people? There are
four methods in which the personnel function can take the lead and
make the most of its opportunity to add value:

1. by generally acting as a change agent, initiating strategies and
   programmes for developing a more positive quality- and performance-orientated culture
2. by making specific contributions in the areas of HR planning,
   resourcing, training and development, performance management, reward and employee relations
3. by ensuring that any personnel initiatives in such fields as
   training and development are treated as investments on which a
   proper return will be obtained which will increase added value
4. by delivering cost-effective personnel services, ie providing
   value for money

Approaches

To put these methods to use the following approaches may be considered:

- Identify critical success factors and focus attention on them.
- Adopt a strategic perspective in managing the HR function.
- Use return-on-investment criteria to determine the viability of HR
  initiatives.
- Conduct a utility analysis.
- Manage the HR department cost-effectively.

Critical success factor analysis

Our research indicated that in the organisations we contacted the process of strategic HRM is based on a clear vision of what the organisation is setting out to achieve supported by well-defined values, goals and corporate/business strategies.

The approach adopted by each organisation was essentially to identify the key issues concerning people which are likely to make the most impact on the organisation's performance. This understanding of the contribution that people can make should emerge directly from an analysis of the critical success factors that contribute to added value. Attention can then be focused on these factors.

In the organisations we visited, the critical success factors varied. At Albion Bank there is a strong emphasis on performance; while the Director of Personnel for Loamshire Council emphasised the importance of change management:

> I see my role as being very much that of anticipating the future and understanding the changing environment, and then assessing the fitness of our organisation to cope with change.

At Megastores it is also the calibre of people which is the key to success. As the Managing Director pointed out:

> We are in the vanguard of retailing. Our net profit to sales ratio is about the highest in the high street and in profit terms we are growing at a faster rate than the market. The biggest challenge will be to maintain that competitive advantage and to do that we need to maintain and continue to attract very high calibre people.

At Motorola, the HR Director suggested:

> The three core competences of the company are technology, quality and people. Motorola can be described as a technology- and quality-driven company which has to invest in people to ensure that it keeps ahead of the market in terms of both technology and quality.

At Pilkington Optronics the emphasis is on competences. As David Roberts, Personnel Director, said:

> We have technical ability, which makes us a winner, and this depends on the competences of our people, which are growing all the time. What is critical to our success is therefore the ability to attract and retain the right calibre of people . . . our HR strategy is basically built around competences.

In Rover Group the emphasis is on quality as the critical success factor. This is very much built into the business strategy, which is completely based on the vision established five years ago that 'the Rover Group will be internationally renowned for extraordinary customer satisfaction'. David Bower, Personnel Director said:

> Total quality improvement in Rover Group is no longer seen as a 'programme' but is at the heart of our corporate philosophy of management. It exercises a strong and increasing influence on day-to-day activities at all levels within the company.

Achieving a strategic perspective in managing HR activities

Achieving added value and competitive advantage through people requires HR activities to be managed from a strategic perspective. The following approaches are suggested by Lengnick-Hall and Lengnick-Hall (1990):

- The aim of the HR function should be defined as the maximisation of corporate profits through the better use and management of people. This statement focuses attention on corporate-wide objectives and directs activities towards results, not just processes.
- HR executives should demonstrate a thorough understanding of the competitive climate, product options, cost constraints, marketing characteristics and all other aspects of productivity and profitability affecting the firm.
- HR professionals must be expected to understand, predict and be

held accountable for the direct and indirect contribution their performance makes to the bottom line.

The 'return on investment' approach

No HR strategy or programme should ever be proposed without considering what return is expected on the investment. This is the approach adopted by Megastores. Tom O'Neill, Managing Director of Pilkington Optronics, found it remarkable that in the past, personnel people would come to him to seek approval for training investments without having made any calculations on the benefits that would, in added value terms, result from them. Why, he asked, should personnel people be immune from the discipline that all other functional managers have to follow? No production manager, for example, would ever make a request for a new machine tool without producing an accounting rate of return or pay-back calculation.

Of course it can be much more difficult for personnel managers to quantify the expected benefits of their initiatives in financial terms. But the attempt should be made wherever possible – for example, by indicating the outcome of an initiative in terms of increased productivity, reduced employee turnover, lower absence rates or a lower incidence of accidents, and attaching financial values to the benefits these outcomes are expected to produce.

This approach can apply to any HR initiative, including the introduction of a performance-management system, training and development programmes, assessment or development centres, competence analysis, performance-related pay or skill-based pay. In the latter areas research conducted by the Institute of Personnel Management (Cannell and Wood, 1992; Cross, 1992) revealed the extent to which new schemes had been launched with high hopes but without calculating what the actual benefits would be or how much they would cost. Michael Cross produced a frightening case-study example of an organisation which had completely underestimated the costs of introducing skill-based pay.

Utility analysis

Utility analysis provides a decision-support framework that explicitly considers the costs and benefits of HR decisions. The aim is to
predict, explain and improve the utility or 'usefulness' of different
HR decisions. It focuses on HR programmes, ie sets of activities or
procedures that affect HR value.

Utility analysis as described by Boudreau (1988) requires:

- a **problem** – a gap between what is desired and what is being
  currently achieved
- a set of **alternatives** to address the problem
- a set of **attributes** – the variables that describe the important
  characteristics of the alternatives (such as effects on productivity,
  costs and employee attitudes)
- a **utility function**, or a system to combine the attributes into an
  overall judgement of each alternative's usefulness

Utility analysis focuses on:

- **quantity** – the effect of work behaviours over time
- **quality** – the production of large improvements or the avoidance
  of large reductions in the quality of those work behaviours
- **cost** – the minimisation of the costs of developing, implementing
  and maintaining programmes

These are, rightly, in line with the factors used by any other function.

It is accepted that all the variables to be assessed may not be
capable of being measured precisely, but uncertainty of this kind
takes place in all aspects of management (eg measuring consumer
preferences).

Utility analysis depends on good management information and
the possible limitations of such information and the costs of collecting it should be recognised. Detailed management information
will only prove useful if it serves the following purposes:

- It is likely to correct decisions that otherwise would have been incorrect.
- The corrections are important and produce large benefits.
- The cost of compiling the information does not outweigh the expected benefit of corrected decisions.

Managing the HR function cost-effectively

Managing the HR function cost-effectively means starting from the premise referred to above that nothing should be carried out by the function unless the costs and benefits of the programme or activity have been properly calculated. It is also necessary to re-examine the role and size of the function. Many organisations, including some of those we visited, are changing the role of the personnel function from a large service-provision agency to one which is primarily concerned with making strategic contributions on policy issues while the members of the function act as internal consultants. The HR function is not and should not be immune from the pressures for downsizing and delayering. More and more, as we established in our research, increased responsibility for human resource management is being placed on line managers. But members of the HR function should still play the important roles of initiators of change and interventionists when key HR issues need to be addressed, and they should take on a coaching role as necessary to help line managers to fulfil their HR responsibilities.

The function may continue to provide basic administrative services concerned with recruitment, training, pay and employee records, but constant attacks must be launched on the costs of running these services and a strategic approach to the computerisation of personnel processes should be part of that campaign.

Conclusions

It is people who create added value and competitive edge. The HR function can play a crucial role in enhancing added value by concentrating on the critical success factors that determine the extent to which the organisation has well-motivated and highly committed people with the required skills, and is able to manage them effectively. In the words of one of the managing directors we met, their essential role is also 'to create an environment in which everyone has the freedom and confidence to maximise their contribution'.

Competitive edge is achieved by innovation, marketing and providing better quality and higher levels of customer service. It is not achieved in the long run simply by cutting costs or prices. The HR function is responsible for working alongside top management to create an organisation and a culture which is conducive to innovation and is dedicated to total quality, while at the same time being aware of the need to maintain cost leadership.

9

 Evaluating the HR Function

The potential for the HR function to play a significant role in increasing added value and achieving competitive advantage may be considerable, as suggested in the last chapter, but how can the effectiveness of the function be measured at both the strategic level and at the level of support and service provision? In a strategic HRM context such measurements have to be made to ensure that an added-value contribution is being made and to indicate where improvements or changes in direction are needed.

Our discussions with chief executives and other directors indicated that the most popular basis for evaluation was their judgements which, from what they said to us, were related to factors such as:

- an understanding of the organisation – its mission, values, critical success factors, product-marketing strategies, technology or method of operation and distinctive competences
- the effectiveness of contributions to top management team decision-making on corporate/business issues
- the extent to which innovatory, realistic and persuasive proposals were made on HR strategies, policies and programmes
- the capacity to deliver as promised
- the quality of the advice and services they provided, assessed mainly in subjective terms – eg, it is practical, it meets my needs, it solves my problem, the services are efficient, the HR function responds quickly to requests for help or advice
- the ability to build and maintain stable and co-operative relationships with trade unions
- the ability to handle difficult situations such as downsizing
- in very general terms, the contribution personnel executives make to developing the corporate culture, their influence on management style and their abilities as facilitators and managers of change

- the overall credibility of the personnel director and his/her ability to work as a full member of the top management team

These largely subjective evaluations were supplemented by the analysis of key employment ratios such as turnover, absenteeism, suggestions received and acted upon, health and safety statistics and the outcome of customer-satisfaction surveys.

In some of the organisations, for example Pilkington Optronics, formal surveys were made of the opinions of line managers about the services they received from the personnel function, and employee attitude surveys were also used as a means of evaluation in organisations such as Pilkington Optronics, Rover Group and Welland Water.

The general impression we gained was that in most of the organisations, evaluations were not made on a particularly systematic basis. However, the precise evaluation of the contribution of the HR function will never be easy, and the adoption of an HRM approach which involves line management having greater responsibility for HR activities makes it even more difficult. In these circumstances, where line management is 'delivering' HRM, the personnel function will be making more of an indirect contribution by taking on a 'partnership' role. This does not mean that the members of the HR function will not be able to exert a powerful influence, as long as they take the initiative in introducing new, relevant and cost-effective HR processes, persuade top management to confront and handle critical HR issues and provide the backing, encouragement, coaching, training and support line managers need if they are to handle complex HR issues and processes successfully.

This problem should not deter anyone from making a determined attempt to measure HR effectiveness, and there are a number of approaches which can be adopted as discussed below.

Overall approach

An important distinction is made by Tsui and Gomez-Mejia (1988) between process criteria – how well things are done – and output criteria – the impact made by the process on organisational and operational performance, ie the effectiveness of the end result. This is broadly the old (Peter Drucker, 1967) distinction between efficiency and effectiveness – ie doing things right in terms of *what* you do (efficiency) rather than doing the right things in terms of the *results* you achieve (effectiveness). In terms of HR effectiveness, it means determining the extent to which HR policies, programmes and practices, and the advice and support provided by the HR function enable line managers to achieve business objectives and meet operational requirements.

When deciding on how the HR function should be evaluated it is also necessary to distinguish between quantitative criteria such as turnover or absenteeism figures, and qualitative criteria such as line managers' opinions of the personnel function or the outcome of employee-attitude surveys.

Types of performance measures

The types of performance measures which can be used to evaluate the personnel function are:

- **money measures,** which include maximising income, minimising expenditure and improving rates of return
- **time measures,** express performance against work timetables, the amount of backlog and speed of activity or response
- **measures of effect,** which include attainment of a standard, changes in behaviour (of colleagues, staff, clients or customers), physical completion of the work and the level of take-up of a service
- **reaction,** which indicates how others judge the function or its members and is therefore a less objective measure. Reaction can be measured by peer assessments, performance ratings by internal or external clients or customers or the analysis of comments and complaints.

Evaluation criteria

It has been suggested by Guest and Peccei (1994) that the effectiveness of HRM can be measured by reference to:

- **organisational effectiveness.** But it may not be possible to separate HR and organisational effectiveness, which will be affected
  by external events, and this approach does not provide a base for
  decisions about HR policy and practice.
- **specified goals.** This is a plausible method, if good measures of
  goal attainment can be used and if allowance is made for unan-
  ticipated events.
- **specified quantified measures.** Labour costs, turnover and productivity have high credibility but may be difficult to interpret
  and can be affected by non-HRM factors and are insufficient on
  their own.
- **stakeholder perspective.** This uses the subjective views of key
  interest groups, eg the Board, on personnel effectiveness and is
  probably the most satisfactory method.

Approaches to evaluation

The main approaches that in practice are adopted by organisations
to evaluate HR effectiveness are:

- *quantitative – macro* (organisational)
- *quantitative – micro* (specified aspects of employee behaviour or
  reaction)
- *quantitative/qualitative* (achievement of specified goals)
- *qualitative – macro* (an overall and largely subjective assessment
  of the HR function)
- *qualitative* (client satisfaction)
- *qualitative* (employee satisfaction)

The last two incorporate Guest and Peccei's criterion of 'stakeholder' perspective.

Organisational quantitative criteria

At organisational level, the quantitative criteria which can be used include:

- added value per employee
- profit per employee
- sales value per employee
- costs per employee
- added value per pound of employment costs

Added value per pound of employment costs was used in two of the research organisations (Pilkington Optronics and Rover Group) and has the advantage of bringing together both benefits (added value) and costs (of employment).

If HRM is the concern of the whole top management team, and of line managers as well as personnel specialists, this provides an interesting general measure of effectiveness. It will not isolate the contribution of the personnel function, but in an HRM culture this would not be so appropriate if the overall impact of strategic HRM is being assessed.

Another reason for using quantified macro-measures as pointed out by Tyson (1985), is that:

> The business objectives become 'sold' as part of the personnel policies. The discipline of sitting down to look at training objectives, for example in terms of sales value or added value, brings out what *can* be assessed and raises the useful question of why we are proposing this programme, if we are unable to relate it to the business.

This approach to assessing HR initiatives and programmes in terms of what they add to the business is central to that adopted by Mega-stores.

Specific quantitative criteria

Specified quantitative criteria can be classified into two categories:

those relating to measurable aspects of employee behaviours and those relating to the type, level and costs of the services provided by the personnel department to its clients.

Employee behaviour criteria

Employee behaviour criteria include:

- employee retention and turnover rates
- absenteeism rate
- ratio of suggestions received to number of employees
- number of usable proposals from quality circles or improvement groups
- cost savings arising from suggestions and/or quality circle recommendations
- frequency/severity rate of accidents
- ratio of grievances to number of employees
- time lost through disputes
- number of references to industrial tribunals on such issues as unfair dismissal, equal opportunity, equal pay, harassment or racial discrimination and the outcome of such references

In some of these areas, eg employee retention and absenteeism rates, the personnel function cannot be held entirely accountable. But it *is* a shared responsibility and the measures will indicate problem areas which may be related to the quality of the advice or services provided by the function.

Personnel department service criteria

The quantifiable criteria available to measure the level and value of service provision by the personnel function include:

- average time to fill vacancies
- time to respond to applicants
- ratio of acceptance to offers made

- cost of advertisements per reply/engagement
- training hours/days per employee
- time to respond to and settle grievances
- cost of induction training per employee
- cost of benefits per employee
- measurable improvements in productivity as a direct result of training
- measurable improvements in individual and organisational performance as a direct result of the operaiton of performance-related pay and performance-management schemes
- ratio of personnel department costs to profit, sales turnover or added value
- personnel costs in relation to budget
- ratio of personnel staff to employees

The usefulness of those measures is variable, as is the practicality of collecting reliable information. Figures on training days per employee do not mean much in themselves unless there is some measure of the relevance and impact of that training. To rely on this measure would be like rewarding sales representatives on the basis of the sales volume they generate rather than the contribution their sales make to profit and fixed costs.

It is also possible that the costs of collecting and analysing some sorts of information may not be justified by the benefits which they could theoretically produce in the shape of improved performance. It is a matter of judgement to select the criteria which are likely to be the most relevant, and this will depend on the circumstances of the organisation and the particular pressures to which it and its personnel function is being subjected. It may be appropriate to highlight some criteria for a period and then, if the problem has been resolved, focus attention on other areas.

Achievement of specified goals

This approach, as used by Rover Group, involves measuring achievements against agreed objectives – this may be the final outcome or a measure of progress towards a goal as indicated by the extent to which specified 'milestones' have been reached.

The specified objectives could be expressed in terms such as:

- all employees to have received training on the implementation of equal opportunities policies by 1 June
- an agreement with the various trade unions to setting up single-table bargaining to be reached by the end of the year
- the competence analysis programme to be completed within 12 months
- salary surveys to be conducted and a report on the implications on salary scales to be submitted by 1 September
- the new performance management system to be fully operational within the next six months

'Project' objectives set along these lines should include some indication of the standard of achievement expected, for example:

> The effectiveness of the performance management system will be judged on:
>
> - an evaluation of user reactions (managers and individuals)
> - an assessment of the quality of the performance review processes
> - an analysis of the outputs of the system in terms of development and improvement plans
> - the number of upheld appeals on assessments
> - the impact the scheme is making on motivation, performance and commitment (as measured by a structured questionnaire to managers and individuals).

An example of this approach is provided by John Towers, Chief Executive of Rover Group. He evaluates the contribution of the personnel function on exactly the same basis as he would that of the areas controlled by any of the other members of his top management team. He invites each part of the organisation to establish the 10 most important things that the function should be doing during the period of the business plan, and particularly the next budget period, as a basis for monitoring and reviewing achievements. In the case of personnel, this would include such matters as employee development or, more specifically, the control of absenteeism. What he looks for are areas in which the personnel function could be influential in ensuring that improvements actually occur.

Subjective overall evaluation

Perhaps the most common method of evaluating the HR function is a subjective assessment by the Chief Executive or the Board which will be related to such general factors as:

- the quality of the advice and services provided as observed or experienced directly by the evaluator
- the degree to which members of the function are proactive rather than reactive (if that is what the management wants, which is not always the case)
- feedback from line managers obtained in a haphazard fashion as to whether or not they think personnel is 'a good thing' and is 'doing a good job'

The dangers or relying on subjective and *ad hoc* measures like these are obvious but they are much used, as our research established.

Systematically collected user reaction measures

Rather than relying on haphazard and highly subjective assessments this approach involves identifying the key criteria for measuring the degree to which clients of the HR function in the shape of directors, managers and team leaders are satisfied with the quality of advice and services they provide.

Areas in which the quality of services provided by the personnel function can be assessed include:

- understanding of strategic business imperatives
- anticipation of business and management needs
- ability to function as a 'business partner' in the team

- quality of advice given in terms of its relevance to the problem or issue, the clarity and conviction with which the advice is given, the practicality of the recommendations
- the quality of the back-up advice and services offered to implement recommendations, the extent to which ultimately the proposals work
- speed of response to requests for advice or services
- promptness in dealing with grievances and appeals
- help to managers in identifying and meeting training needs
- extent to which training and development programmes meet company/individual needs
- delivery of advice and services which make a significant impact on improving the quality and performance of staff
- development of programmes and processes which address short- and long-term business needs, which are 'owned' by line managers, and which produce the anticipated impact on motivation, commitment and performance.

Assessments of the contribution of the personnel function in areas such as those listed above can be made by conducting surveys of client opinion.

Employee satisfaction measures

The degree to which the employee stakeholders are satisfied with personnel policies and practices as they affect them can be measured by attitude surveys which obtain opinions and perceptions of employees on:

- the extent to which they believe promotion, job-evaluation, performance-appraisal, performance-related pay and grievance processes and procedures operate fairly
- the degree to which they are satisfied with pay and benefits
- the extent to which they feel they are involved in decisions that affect them
- how well they feel they are kept informed on matters of importance to them

- the consistency with which personnel policies concerning pay, equal opportunity etc are applied
- the opportunities available to them for training and development
- the degree to which their work makes the best use of their skills and abilities
- the extent to which they are clear about what is expected of them
- the support and guidance they receive from their managers and team leaders
- their working environment from the point of view of health and safety, and the general conditions under which they work
- the facilities (restaurant, car parking etc) with which they are provided
- generally, the climate and management style of the organisation

Individual evaluation

The evaluation approaches listed above are directed at both the personnel function as a whole and its individual members. But it is also necessary specifically to agree the overall objectives and standards of performance expected from members of the function as a basis for assessment. The following is an example of a list of standards of performance agreed for a personnel manager:

1. A proactive approach is consistently adopted in making proposals to management on the development of HR policies and practices which will improve business performance and add value.
2. Realistic plans are made to anticipate future staff requirements and avoid skill shortages or unmanageable staff surpluses.
3. Systematic recruitment and selection procedures are maintained which provide a wholly acceptable service to line managers. An acceptable service is one that includes:

   - a prompt (within one working day) response to requests for advice or help in recruitment
   - the delivery of acceptable job descriptions, person specifications, draft advertisements and media plans within three working days

- the use of psychometric tests which have been properly evaluated, are administered by trained staff and provide valuable insights for selection purposes
- the delivery of a shortlist of candidates by an agreed deadline who meet the specification, supported by helpful profiles

4. Good advice is given on employment and health and safety matters which is based on a thorough understanding of the relevant legislation and company policies and procedures. The advice is such that the company is not involved in any tribunal or other form of legal action.

5. Performance management is introduced by the end of the year, the pilot tests having shown that the approach is acceptable to managers and staff and full briefing and training programmes having taken place.

6. Training programmes are based on a systematic analysis of needs and meet success criteria as established by programme and course evaluations.

7. Reward-management policies and practices are developed which ensure that rewards are both competitive and equitable and contribute to the attraction, motivation and retention of staff within cost budgets. Reward reviews are conducted efficiently (ie on time and accurately) and managers are provided with practical and helpful advice on their responsibilities for managing rewards in their departments.

8. A good climate of employee relations is maintained as indicated by the outcomes of employee-attitude surveys and the absence of disputes or references to the grievance procedure.

9. The computerised personnel information system is used to maintain accurate records and to generate information for HR planning and decision-making purposes.

Benchmarking

The methods of measuring personnel effectiveness listed above all rely on collecting and analysing internal data and opinions. But it is also desirable to 'benchmark', ie compare what the personnel function is doing within the organisation with what is happening elsewhere. This will involve gaining information on 'best practice' which, even if it is not transferable in total to the organisation conducting the survey, should at least provide information on areas for development or improvement. A number of the organisations we visited, such as Pilkington Optronics, Rover Group and Megastores were adopting this approach to assist them in achieving 'world-class' levels of performance.

Preferred approach

Every organisation will develop its own approach to evaluating the effectiveness of the personnel function and its members. There are no standard measures, and our survey organisations provided examples of each of the methods described in this chapter.

Perhaps, as Guest and Peccei (1994) suggest:

> The most sensible and the most important indicator of HRM effectiveness will be the judgements of key stakeholders . . . The political, stakeholder, perspective on effectiveness in organizations acknowledges that it is the interpretation placed on quantified results and the attributions of credit and blame that are derived from them that matter most in judging effectiveness. In other words, at the end of the day, it is always the qualitative interpretations by those in positions of power that matter most.

But they recognised 'the desirability of also developing clearly specified goals and quantitative indicators, together with financial criteria'.

10

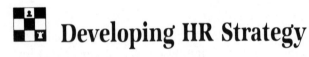 **Developing HR Strategy**

The development process

The process of developing HR strategies involves generating strategic HRM options and then making appropriate strategic choices. These choices should, so far as possible:

- relate to but also anticipate the needs of the organisation
- have the capacity to change the character and direction of the organisation
- equip the organisation to deal effectively with the external pressures and demands affecting it
- focus on areas of critical need, ie the critical success factors of the organisation (the identification of critical success factors does not, of course, tell you what the HR strategy should be but it does help to focus on the key issues or 'drivers' of organisational and individual performance).
- answer fundamental questions such as 'What is constraining us?' and 'What is stopping us from delivering results?'
- be founded on detailed analysis and study, not just wishful thinking
- incorporate the experienced and collective judgement of top management
- provide for the acquisition and development of people with the skills needed to manage and sustain the organisation in the future to meet organisational objectives
- be composed of components which fit with and support each other
- be capable of being turned into actionable programmes

A model for developing HR strategies

Essentially, the formulation of HR strategy requires answers to just three questions:

1. Where are we now?
2. Where do we want to be in one, two, three or even five years' time?
3. How are we going to get there?

But it is more complicated than that and the process could be modelled as shown in Figure 10.1.

Figure 10.1
A sequential strategic HRM model

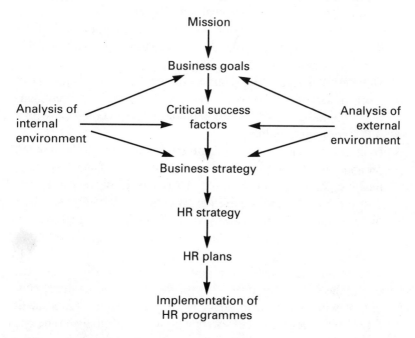

This, broadly, is the approach used by Rover Group. But the process does not need to be expressed as formally as this. It is perfectly possible to develop a clearly articulated HR strategy without documenting it quite so thoroughly, as the other organisations covered by the research demonstrated.

A systematic approach

There is, however, much to be said for adopting a systematic approach to formulating HR strategies which considers all the relevant organisational, business and environmental issues, and a methodology for this purpose was developed by Dyer and Holder (1988) as follows:

1. **Assess feasibility.** From an HR point of view, feasibility depends on whether the numbers and types of key people required to make the proposal succeed can be obtained on a timely basis and at a reasonable cost and whether the behavioural expectations assumed by the strategy (eg retention rates and productivity levels) are realistic.
2. **Determine desirability.** Examine the implications of strategy in terms of sacrosanct HR policies (eg a strategy of rapid retrenchment would have to be called into question by a company with a full-employment policy).
3. **Determine goals.** These indicate the main issues to be worked on and they derive primarily from the content of the corporate/business strategy. For example, a strategy to become a lower-cost producer would require the reduction of labour costs. This in turn translates into two types of HR goals: higher performance standards (contribution) and reduced headcounts (composition).
4. **Decide means of achieving goals.** The general rule is that the closer the external and internal fit, the better the strategy, consistent with the need to adapt flexibly to change. External fit refers to the degree of consistency between HR goals on the one hand and the exigencies of the underlying corporate/business strategy and relevant environmental conditions on the other. Internal fit measures the extent to which HR means follow from HR ends or goals and other relevant environmental conditions, as well as the degree of coherence or synergy among the various HR means.

In addition the HR strategist should take pains to understand the levels at which corporate/business strategies are formed, the critical success factors of the organisation and the style it adopts in creating strategies and monitoring their implementation. It will then be easier to focus on those corporate or business unit issues which are likely to have HR implications.

Key issues

The key issues which may impact on HR strategies include:

- intentions concerning growth or retrenchment, acquisitions, mergers, divestments, diversification, product/market development
- proposals on increasing competitive advantage or organisational effectiveness through higher levels of productivity, improved quality/customer service, cost reduction (downsizing)
- the felt need to develop a more positive, performance-orientated culture
- any other culture-management imperatives associated with changes in the philosophies of the organisation in such areas as gaining commitment, mutuality, communications, involvement, empowerment, devolution, team working and developing a 'climate of success'.
- any external environmental factors (opportunities and threats) which may impinge on the organisation such as government interventions, UK or European legislation, competition, economic pressures (recession)

Corporate strategies in these areas may be influenced by HR factors but not excessively so. HR strategies are, after all, about making corporate/business strategies work. But the corporate strategy must take into account key HR opportunities and constraints.

Corporate strategy sets the agenda for HR strategy in the following areas:

- HR mission
- values, culture and style
- organisational philosophy and approach to the management of people
- top management as a corporate resource
- resourcing
- skills acquisition and development
- commitment
- productivity
- performance management
- rewards
- employee relations

Integrating corporate and HR strategies

When considering how to integrate corporate and HR strategies the starting point should be the belief that they are inseparable – corporate strategies cannot be conceived without paying attention to HR considerations and HR strategies have to flow from the main strategic thrusts and values of the organisation. It should be noted that in establishing these links, account must be taken of the fact that strategies for change have also to be integrated with changes in the external and internal environments. An excessive pursuit of 'fit' with the status quo will inhibit the flexibility of approach which is essential in turbulent conditions.

As suggested by Cooke and Armstrong (1990), to achieve a link in rigorous terms requires a means of quantifying the additional resources allocated to HR overall and at the level of each element of HR strategy, and measuring and comparing the marginal return on investing in each element. But this approach is unlikely to be practicable. The link must therefore be judgemental, but it could still be fairly rigorous. Conceptually, the approach would be to develop a matrix as illustrated in Figure 10.2, which for each of the key elements of business strategy identifies the associated key elements of HR strategy.

Figure 10.2

A conceptual approach to linking business and HR strategies

	Market development	Product development	New technology	Acquisitions mergers divestments
Organisation				
Resourcing				
HRD				
Performance management				
Reward				
Employee relations				

Even if the approach cannot be as rigorous as this, the principle of considering each key area of corporate strategy and, reciprocally, the HR implications, provides a useful basis for integration.

Questions to be answered

The questions to which answers are required when formulating HR strategies include:

- What is the nature of the corporate culture? Does it help or hinder the achievement of the organisation's goals?
- What needs to be done to define or redefine our values in such areas as quality, customer service, innovation, team working, empowerment and the responsibility of the organisation for its employees?

- What do we need to do to increase commitment? How do we communicate our intentions and achievements to employees and what steps do we take to obtain feedback from them and to involve them in organisational affairs?
- What kind of skills and competences do we need in the future?
- Are performance levels high enough to meet demands for increased profitability, higher productivity, better quality and improved customer service?
- Will the organisation's structure and systems be able to cope with future challenges in their present form?
- Are we making the best use of the skills and capacities of our employees?
- Are we investing enough in developing those skills and capacities?
- Are there any potential constraints in the form of skills shortages or industrial relations problems?
- Have we serious problems in attracting and retaining key employees? If so, what are the causes (eg uncompetitive levels of pay or an inequitable pay structure)?
- Are our employment costs too high?
- Is there any scope/need for delayering or downsizing?
- How stable are our relationships with trade unions?
- Do we need to establish a new relationship with the trade unions?

The answers to these and similar questions define the areas in which HR strategies need to be developed. The important thing is to give an overall sense of purpose to HR activities by linking them explicitly to the needs of the organisation and its employees. The factors to be taken into account when developing and implementing a strategic HRM approach are set out in the Appendix.

Achieving coherence

The concept of coherence in strategic HRM, as described in Chapter 3, emphasises the need to develop a mutually reinforcing and interlinked set of personnel policies and programmes which jointly contribute to the achievement of organisational goals.

Coherence is an ideal which may be difficult to attain unless you are starting from scratch, for example, on a greenfield site. To have a 'grand design' may be highly desirable, but in rapidly changing circumstances, when there will always be an element of fire-fighting in dealing with people issues, the 'big picture' will not remain the same. New initiatives will be required and the pieces may not always fit as neatly into the jigsaw as one would like.

Coherence is most likely to be achieved, as indicated by our research (see Chapter 6) when there is strongly developed strategic thrust which is driven by the whole top management team and which provides the framework into which can be fitted interrelated personnel programmes and processes. If, for example, the drive is for improved performance, a coherent and interlocking set of programmes can be developed making use of such processes as competence profiling and performance management which feed into one another so that the same competence frameworks are used for selection, performance appraisal, management development and reward.

Coherence can be developed by considering systematically how different inputs can be combined to contribute to the achievement of desired outcomes. This process is illustrated in Figure 10.3.

Getting into action

Because strategies tend to be expressed as abstractions, they must be translated into programmes with clearly stated objectives and deliverables. But getting strategies into action is not easy. The term 'strategic HRM' has been devalued in some quarters; sometimes it means no more than a few generalised ideas about personnel policies, at other times it describes a short-term plan, eg to increase the retention rate of graduates. It must be emphasised that HR strategies are not just programmes, policies, or plans concerning personnel issues which the personnel department happens to find

Figure 10.3
A conceptual approach to developing coherent HR programmes

OUTPUTS	competence profiling	performance management	organisation development	education/ continuous learning
resourcing	*			*
performance	*	*	*	*
quality		*	*	*
teamwork		*	*	*
empowerment			*	*

INPUTS

important. Piecemeal and unrelated initiatives do not constitute strategy.

Strategic HRM as an attitude of mind

Although systematic approaches such as those described above are necessary, it should be remembered that strategic HRM is more of an attitude of mind than a step-by-step process which takes you inexorably from a mission statement to implementation.

Strategic HR planning is usually a much less orderly affair than the models suggest. This is entirely understandable if it is borne in mind that strategic HRM is as much about the management of change in conditions of uncertainty as about the rigorous development and implementation of a logical plan.

Perhaps the best way to look at the reality of strategic HRM is to remember Mintzberg's (1978) statement that strategy formulation is about 'preferences, choices, and matches' rather than an exercise 'in applied logic'. It is also desirable to follow Mintzberg's analysis and treat HR strategy as a perspective rather than a rigorous procedure for mapping the future. As Moore (1992) points out, Mintzberg has looked inside the organisation, indeed inside the heads of the collective strategists, and come to the conclusion that, relative to the organisation, strategy is analogous to the personality of an individual. As Mintzberg sees them, all strategies exist in the minds of those people they make an impact upon. What is important is that people in the organisation share the same perspective 'through their intentions and/or by their actions'. This is what Mintzberg calls the collective mind, and reading that mind is essential if we are 'to understand how intentions . . . become shared, and how action comes to be exercised on a collective yet consistent basis'.

No one else has made this point so well as Mintzberg and what our research revealed is that strategic HRM *is* being practised in the organisations we visited in the Mintzbergian sense. In other words *intentions* are shared amongst the top team and this leads to actions being exercised on a *collective yet consistent basis*. In each case the shared intentions emerged as a result of strong leadership from the chief executive with the other members of the top team acting *jointly* in pursuit of well-defined goals. These goals indicated quite clearly the critical success factors of competence, commitment, performance, contribution and quality which drive the HR strategy.

Prescriptions for success

The only prescription that can safely be offered for the successful development and implementation of strategic HRM is that there should be a closely knit top team, which includes a personnel director who plays a full part in business discussions and in making choices on business strategy. This team should provide visionary leadership and operate on a collegiate basis. Our research suggested that while some of the impetus will come from the chief executive and the personnel director, the other members can and do play an equally important part in forming the 'declarations of intent' which provide the basis for HR strategies.

The role of the personnel director in this context is clearly that of understanding the strategic business imperatives of the organisation and the changing environment in which it exists. The personnel director has to take account of the wants and needs of the various stakeholders in the organisation. He or she must understand its culture, climate and management style and be aware of how they may need to be changed in order to meet future challenges and opportunities. Clearly, the personnel director must remember Hamel and Prahalad's (1989) dictum that strategy is about maintaining strategic fit between resources and opportunities.

Conclusion

HR strategy contributes to the business strategy but is also justified by it. The aim should be to make it bold, imaginative, innovative, clear and actionable. It must also be selective – focusing on priorities – and flexible – rapidly adjusting to change. HR strategy should be formulated by a continuous process of analysing what is happening to the organisation and where it is going.

It is sometimes suggested that HR plans should be entirely contingent on the circumstances of the organisation. But this seems to limit any breakthroughs – the development of new paradigms about how the organisation can function even more effectively than before. When developing HR strategies the aim should be to establish new directions, not just to smooth the way along the present path.

The vital point to remember about HR strategy is that it should give an overall sense of purpose to HR activities which can provide the people the organisation needs and help them to understand where they are going, how they are going to get there, why certain things are happening, and most importantly, the contribution they are expected to make towards securing the organisation's future.

♟ Conclusion: How Much Reality?

On reading the literature we sometimes formed the impression that the concept of strategic HRM was invented by academics for academics. The rhetoric of strategic HRM as they present it does not seem to relate to what actually happens in offices, factories, shops and distribution depots. Perhaps they agree with T. S. Eliot: 'Go go go said the bird, human kind cannot bear very much reality.'

Certainly, none of the chief executives, managing directors and other directors we met ever referred to what they were doing as 'strategic HRM'. They were just getting on with whatever they felt was best for their organisation. It so happens that much of what they do corresponds with the academic prescriptions for strategic HRM but that is because it suits their purpose, not because they are putting an HRM model into practice.

The point is that it does not matter a jot whether it is referred to as strategic HRM, HR strategy or people strategy, or even if the word strategy is not mentioned at all, just as it does not matter whether it is called HR management or personnel management. What is important is that a strategic, integrated and coherent approach is adopted to the development of policies which will address longer-term issues concerning the management and employment of people. Nor does it matter a bit whether or not the strategy (or whatever it is called) has been written down or has emerged in the form of a clear understanding of the broad intentions of management concerning its personnel policies and programmes. Some of the organisations involved in our research had written down their strategies; others had not. But we could not detect any significant differences between them in terms of clarity of purpose, mutual understanding amongst the top team of the direction in which the organisation should go, the degree to which business and HR strategies are integrated, or the ability of the organisation to convert its plans into effective action.

The reality of strategic HRM is that it does not and cannot exist

186

except as a concept – a notion of how longer-term HR issues should be managed, an attitude of mind, an approach, a 'pattern in a stream of activities', a perspective. It should not be prescribed as a standardised set of practices which will transform organisations overnight. You cannot say, 'Let's have strategic HRM tomorrow.' It is not, in William Deming's (1982) phrase about TQM, 'instant pudding'. If strategic HRM happens at all it will be an evolutionary process, although it may be accelerated by the pressure of change. A strategic HRM approach only becomes 'real' when it provides the basis for integrated HR strategies which clearly declare the future intentions of the organisation about its people, which are put into effect, and which *work*. And this, on the whole, is what we observed happening in the organisations covered by our research.

The lessons from the research

What our research showed was that strategic approaches to personnel management have been adopted by a number of disparate organisations although, inevitably, these approaches vary considerably. But there are lessons to be learned from each organisation about how personnel strategies can be developed successfully as described in Chapter 4.

The research referred to elsewhere in this book by Guest and Peccei (1994), Guest and Hogue (1994) and Gennard and Kelly (unpublished) has shown that a number of organisations are successfully adopting practices which could broadly be categorised as strategic HRM. This refutes the often repeated canard that HRM only exists in a tiny number of foreign-owned exemplar organisations such as Hewlett Packard, IBM and Japanese electronic or motor-manufacturing firms.

A recent survey by Warwick and Sheffield Universities (Purcell, 1994) revealed that when a personnel director is on the Board the following things, amongst others, are likely to happen:

- Corporate personnel is much more likely to be fully involved in career development and senior management pay decisions and in making decisions about pay assumptions in business-unit budgets.
- The function is more likely to play a part in performance and productivity improvement activity, a classic bottom-line activity.
- The function is also more likely to be a party to strategies for corporate change.
- The organisation is more likely to use four or more methods to communicate company policy to employees, to allow for systems of upward communication, and to recognise trade unions in most, but not all, of its establishments.

But it cannot be inferred from these research projects that such practices are widespread. The Warwick/Sheffield study found that only 30 per cent of the largest companies, with 1,000 or more employees, had a personnel director on the Board, although the Price Waterhouse and Cranfield research (Brewster and Smith, 1990) established that two-thirds of UK organisations employing more than 200 people had a personnel director.

Research carried out in Ireland by Monks (1992) showed that nine out of the 97 organisations fell into the category of 'innovative/sophisticated', ie personnel issues were integrated into strategic plans and personnel was represented on the Board. About one-third of the organisations were in the traditional/administrative category, which roughly corresponds to the Tyson and Fell (1986) 'clerk of works' model, or what Storey (1992) somewhat condescendingly refers to as 'handmaidens'. A further one-fifth of the Irish organisations were in the traditional/industrial relations category, which is equivalent to the Tyson and Fell 'contracts manager' model. No comparable data exists for the UK but it can reasonably be assumed that by far the largest proportion of organisations (say 70 per cent or more) are not practising anything which remotely resembles strategic HRM. Probably these are the organisations which are entirely concerned with short-term financial and product-market issues. The importance of the contribution of people may be recognised but the longer-term considerations are not taken into account to any great extent. In these organisations the personnel function will have a service, support and administrative role; it will not operate strategically.

The conditions required for strategic HRM

The reality of strategic HRM is that it will only be practised in organisations and by personnel directors with a high proportion of the characteristics set out below – these are based on conclusions reached from our research and the research conducted by Armstrong (1989).

Characteristics of organisations which adopt a strategic approach to HRM

Organisations which are most likely to adopt a strategic approach to HRM will have:

- strong, visionary leadership
- a well-developed mission, and well-understood values supporting that mission, especially in the areas of quality, continuous improvement, flexibility, teamwork, performance, involvement, the acceptance of employees as stakeholders and the importance of recognising individual needs
- a closely knit team at the top
- a coherent and clearly articulated business strategy
- a proactive approach to dealing with problems and opportunities but having the capacity to adapt quickly to change
- a clear and separate identity and culture, and involvement in the production and marketing of a single product or related group of products, or the provision of services within one well-defined area
- a personnel director on the Board who is actively involved as a 'business partner' and who is supported by personnel specialists who also take the business-partner role
- line managers who 'own' the HR strategies

- trade unions which are prepared to take on a partnership role
- an appreciation on the part of management that HR strategies are an integral part of corporate/business strategies and that the latter will not be successful unless the human factor and the needs of the various stakeholders are taken into account at the time when strategic decisions are being made

Characteristics of effective personnel/HR directors

Personnel directors who will most probably play a full strategic role as business partners are likely to be:

- very much part of the top management team
- involved in corporate/business planning and the integration of human resource plans with corporate/business plans
- well placed to exert influence on the way in which the enterprise is organised, managed and staffed – all with a view to helping it achieve its strategic objectives
- professionally competent in personnel techniques, although their contribution and credibility will depend mainly on their business awareness and skills and their ability to play a full part as members of the top team
- involved in resourcing at top and senior levels and in so doing be in a strong position to improve organisational effectiveness and, therefore, bottom-line performance
- able to convince others of the need for change and to act as champions of change and as effective change agents
- involved in shaping corporate culture and values
- fully aware of the needs to develop a vision of what the personnel function exists to do, to define its mission, to provide leadership and guidance to the members of the personnel function (without getting over-involved in day-to-day personnel matters) and to maintain the quality of the support the function provides to line managers
- enablers and facilitators, but ones who are well placed to make a significant contribution to end results by adopting an innovatory approach to the improvement of organisational effectiveness and

by intervening as necessary on any matters where there are HR implications which will affect performance

- essentially pragmatists who know about the theory of HRM but also know what is right for their organisation and what will work there.

The future

These requirements are exacting and it is hardly surprising that a large proportion of organisations will not meet them. What our research has shown, however, is that some form of strategic HRM can be practised successfully in widely different organisations. It may not be called strategic HRM and it will operate in a diversity of ways, but it will be there all the same as an approach to managing human resources strategically, although not necessarily as a set of well-defined and systematic practices.

A pessimistic, if realistic, view of the future is that the majority of organisations will continue to survive, even thrive, without the perceived benefit of strategic HRM. And who can say that in the circumstances in which these organisations exist, strategic HRM, as usually defined, would necessarily be relevant?

However, our research led us to the more optimistic conclusion that some form of strategic approach to HR will become increasingly recognised as valid in organisations which are being subjected to ever-greater competitive pressures to improve their performance, and where it becomes evident that this can be achieved by adopting a more strategic and integrated approach to the management of people.

Appendix

▣ Guidelines on Developing a Strategic HRM Approach

1. Get to know and thoroughly understand:
   - the vision of the chief executive on the future of the organisation
   - the views of each of the key directors or top executives concerning the future of their own functions and the challenges and problems facing them
   - the mission of the organisation, whether or not it has been formalised
   - the values of the organisation as espoused and practised
   - the management style of the chief executive and your colleagues
   - the distinctive core competences of the organisation and its people
   - the critical success factors of the organisation
   - the opportunities and threats facing the organisation
   - the objectives of the organisation in terms of rate and direction of growth, quantified wherever possible
   - the measures used by the organisation to assess its performance
   - the corporate or business strategies of the organisation in such areas as:
     - innovation
     - product-market development
     - technological development
     - expansion or downsizing
     - acquisitions, mergers or divestments
2. Develop this understanding by:
   - absorbing and analysing information at board and other meetings or incorporated in any documents which are available or can somehow be obtained
   - playing a full part in board meetings on any corporate or business matters on which you think you can make a contribution

   based on your own knowledge of the challenges and choices
   facing the organisation – bearing in mind that you may be
   able to bring a fresh perspective to these discussions
   - talking informally to your chief executive and your col-
     leagues about their business or functional plans and prob-
     lems, not confining yourself to purely HR issues – your
     credibility and ability to contribute will increase if you show
     an intelligent interest in what is going on and in what may
     transpire in the future
3. Conduct your own analysis of the HR issues which emerge
   from your understanding of the corporate or business issues
   concerning the organisation as a whole or those relating to specific areas. This could be conducted in the form of a SWOT
   (strengths and weaknesses and opportunities and threats)
   analysis. The outcome of this analysis could be grouped under
   headings such as:
   - organisation
   - skill acquisition or expansion
   - competence development
   - continuous learning and development
   - performance improvement
   - values and management style
   - quality and customer service
   - motivation and reward
   - commitment
   - teamwork
   - flexibility
   - participation
   - empowerment
   - employee and trade union relations
   - change management generally
4. Consider any innovations you think are required under any of
   the above headings.
5. Conduct a thorough assessment of these possible strategic
   innovations under such headings as:
   - how they will provide for added value or competitive advan-
     tage

- how they will address the critical strategic issues facing the organisation and fit organisational requirements
- the specific impact they will make on performance and the ability of the organisation to achieve its immediate and longer-term goals
- their costs as well as their benefits
- the financial return you expect from investing in them
- the arguments that are most likely to convince your colleagues that the innovation will pay off (anticipate objections)
- how the innovations will be developed and implemented (the resources and time required)

6. Identify any champions for change in the organisation who are likely to be your allies.
7. Identify any enemies of change who may block your proposals, and decide what to do about them.
8. Test other people's opinions about your ideas.
9. Lobby as necessary (not all key decisions are made in board meetings).
10. Always keep in mind the objectives you are aiming to achieve, how these will support the achievement of organisational objectives and how you are going to ensure that your strategies will be accepted and implemented effectively.

 # Bibliography

ANDREWS, K. A. (1987) *The Concept of Corporate Strategy*, Georgetown, Ontario, Irwin.

ANSOFF, H. I. (1987) *Corporate Strategy*, New York, McGraw-Hill.

ARGYRIS, C. (1957) *Personality and Organization*, New York, Harper & Row.

ARMSTRONG, M. (1987) 'Human resource management: a case of the emperor's new clothes', *Personnel Management*, August, pp 30–5.

ARMSTRONG, M. (1989) *Personnel and the Bottom Line*, London, Institute of Personnel Management.

ARMSTRONG, M. (1991) *A Handbook of Personnel Management Practice* (4th edition), London, Kogan Page.

ARMSTRONG, P. (1989) 'Limits and possibilities for HRM in an age of management accountancy'. In J. Storey, (ed.) *New Perspectives in Human Resource Management*, London, Routledge.

BARNARD, C. (1938) *The Functions of an Executive*, Boston, Mass., Harvard University Press.

BEER, M., SPECTOR, B., LAWRENCE, P., QUINN MILLS, D. and WALTON, R. (1984) *Managing Human Assets*, New York, The Free Press.

BLANCHARD, K. and JOHNSON, S. (1983) *The One Minute Manager*, London, Willow Books.

BLYTON, P. and TURNBULL, P. (eds.) (1992) *Reassessing Human Resource Management*, London, Sage Publications.

BOUDREAU, J. W. (1988) 'Utility analysis', in L. Dyer (ed.) *Human Resource Management: Evolving Roles and Responsibilities*, Washington DC, Bureau of National Affairs.

BOWER, J. L. (1982) 'Business policy in the 1980s', *Academy of Management Review*, Vol. 7 No. 4, pp 630–8.

ℵ BOXALL, P. F. (1992) 'Strategic HRM: a beginning, a new theoretical direction', *Human Resource Management Journal*, Vol. 2 No. 3, pp 61–79.

BOXALL, P. F. (1993) 'The significance of human resource management: a reconsideration of the evidence', *The International Journal of Human Resource Management*, Vol. 4 No. 3 pp 645–65.

ⲭ BOXALL, P. (1994) 'Placing HR strategy at the heart of the business', *Personnel Management*, July, pp 32–5.

BREWSTER, C. (1993) 'Developing a "European" model of human resource management', *International Journal of Human Resource Management*, Vol. 4 No. 4, pp 765–84.

BREWSTER, C. and HOLT LARSEN, H. (1992) 'Human resource management in Europe: evidence from ten countries', *International Journal of Human Resource Management*, Vol. 3 No. 3, pp 409–34.

BREWSTER, C. and SMITH, C. (1990) 'Corporate strategy: a no-go area for personnel?', *Personnel Management*, July, pp 36–40.

BROOKLYN DERR, C., WOOD, J. D., JONES, C. and DUPRES, C. (1993) *The Emerging Role of the Personnel/HR Manager: A United Kingdom and Irish Perspective*, London, Institute of Personnel Management.

CANNELL, M. and WOOD, S. (1992) *Incentive Pay: Impact and Evolution*, London, Institute of Personnel Management.

CHANDLER, A. D. (1962) *Strategy and Structure*, Boston, Mass., MIT Press.

COOKE, R. and ARMSTRONG, M. (1990) 'Towards strategic HRM', *Personnel Management*, December, pp 30–3.

COULSON-THOMAS, C. (1991) 'What the personnel director can bring to the board table', *Personnel Management*, October, pp 36–9.

CROSS, M. (1992) *Skill-based Pay: A Guide for Practitioners*, London, Institute of Personnel Management.

DEMING, W. E. (1982) *Quality, Productivity and Competitive Position*, Cambridge, Mass., MIT Centre for Advanced Engineering Study.

DIGMAN, L. A. (1990) *Strategic Management – Concepts, Decisions, Cases*, Georgetown, Ontario, Irwin.

DRUCKER, P. E. (1955) *The Practice of Management*, London, Heinemann.

DRUCKER, P. E. (1967) *The Effective Executive*, London, Heinemann.

DYER, L. (1984) 'Studying human resource strategy: an approach and an agenda', *Industrial Relations*, Vol. 23 No. 2, pp 156–69.

DYER, L. and HOLDER, G. W. (1988) 'Strategic human resource management and planning', in L. Dyer (ed.) *Human Resource Management: Evolving Roles and Responsibilities*, Washington DC, Bureau of National Affairs.

EAGLETON, T. (1983) *Literary Theory*, Oxford, Blackwell.

EAPM/IMD Survey (1992) 'Personnel function at a crossroads', *Personnel Management*, July, p 5.

FAULKNER, D. and JOHNSON, G. (1992) *The Challenge of Strategic Management*, London, Kogan Page.

FERNIE, S., METCALF, D. and WOODLAND, S. (1994) *Does HRM Boost Employee-Management Relations?*, London, Centre for Economic Performance and Industrial Relations Department, London School of Economics.

FOMBRUN, C. J., TICHY, N. M. and DEVANNA, M. A. (1984) *Strategic Human Resource Management*, New York, Wiley.

FOWLER, A. (1987) 'When chief executives discover HRM', *Personnel Management*, January, p 3.

GILES, E. and WILLIAMS, R. (1991) 'Can the personnel department survive quality management?' *Personnel Management*, April, pp 21–3.

GOOLD, M. and CAMPBELL, A. (1986) *Strategies and Styles: The Role of the Centre in Managing Diversified Corporations*, Oxford, Blackwell.

GUEST, D. E. (1987) 'Human resource management and industrial relations', *Journal of Management Studies*, Vol. 14 No. 5, pp 503–21.

GUEST, D. E. (1989a) 'Human resource management: its implications for industrial relations and trade unions'. In J. Storey, (ed.) *New Perspectives in Human Resource Management*, London, Routledge.

GUEST, D. E. (1989b) 'Personnel and HRM: can you tell the difference?' *Personnel Management*, January, pp 48–51.

GUEST, D. E. (1990) 'Human resource management and the American dream', *Journal of Management Studies*, Vol. 27 No. 4, pp 378–97.

GUEST, D. E. (1991) 'Personnel management: the end of orthodoxy', *British Journal of Industrial Relations*, Vol. 29 No. 2, pp 149–76.

GUEST, D. E. (1992) 'Human resource management in the UK'. In B. Towers (ed.) *The Handbook of Human Resource Management*, Oxford, Blackwell.

GUEST, D. E. and HOGUE, K. (1994) as reported in *Personnel Management Plus*, May, p 1.

GUEST, D. E. and PECCEI, R. (1994) 'The nature and causes of effective human resource management', *British Journal of Industrial Relations*, Vol. 32 No. 2, pp 219–42.

GUNNIGLE, P. and MOORE, S. (1994) 'Linking business strategy and human resource management: issues and implications', *Personnel Review*, Vol. 23 No. 1, pp 63–83.

HAMEL, G. and PRAHALAD, C. K. (1989) 'Strategic intent', *Review*, May–June, pp 63–76.

HAMERMESH, R. G. (1986) *Making Strategy Work – How Senior Managers Produce Results*, New York, Wiley.

HELLER, R. (1972) *The Naked Manager*, London, Barrie & Jenkins.

HENDRY, C. and PETTIGREW, A. (1986) 'The practice of strategic human resource management', *Personnel Review*, 15, pp 2–8.

HENDRY, C. and PETTIGREW, A. (1990) 'Human resource management: an agenda for the 1990s', *International Journal of Human Resource Management*, Vol. 1 No. 3, pp 17–43.

HERZBERG, F. W., MAUSNER, B. and SNYDERMAN, B. (1957) *The Motivation to Work*, New York, Wiley.

HICKSON, D. G., GRAY, D., MALLORY, D. and WILSON, D. (1986) *Top Decisions: Strategic Decision Making in Organizations*, Oxford, Blackwell.

HILL, C. W. and PICKERING, J. F. (1986) 'Divisionalisation, decentralisation and performance of large United Kingdom companies', *Journal of Management Studies*, Vol. 23 No. 1, pp 42–58.

HOFER, C. W. and SCHENDEL, D. (1986) *Strategy Formulation: Analytical Concepts*, New York, West Publishing.

IBM/TOWERS PERRIN (1992) *Priorities for Competitive Advantage*, New York, Towers Perrin.

JOHNSON, G. (1987) *Strategic Change and the Management Process*, Oxford, Blackwell.

KANTER, R. M. (1984) *The Change Masters*, London, Allen & Unwin.

KANTER, R. M. (1989) *When Giants Learn to Dance*, London, Simon & Schuster.

KEENOY, T. (1990a) 'HRM: a case of the wolf in sheep's clothing', *Personnel Review*, Vol. 19 No. 2, pp 3–9.

KEENOY, T. (1990b) 'HRM: rhetoric, reality and contradiction', *International Journal of Human Resource Management*, Vol. 1 No. 3, pp 363–84.

KEENOY, T. and ANTHONY, P. (1992) 'HRM: metaphor, meaning and morality'. In P. Blyton and P. Turnbull (eds.) *Reassessing Human Resource Management*, London, Sage Publications.

KIRKBRIDE, P. S., DURCAN, J. and OBENG, E. D. (1994) 'Change in a chaotic post-modern world', *Journal of Strategic Change*, Vol. 3, pp 151–163.

LEGGE, K. (1978) *Power, Innovation and Problem Solving in Personnel Management*, Maidenhead, McGraw-Hill.

LEGGE, K. (1987) 'Women in personnel management: uphill climb or downhill slide?' In A. Spencer and D. Podmore (eds.) *Women in a Man's World*, London, Tavistock Publications.

LEGGE, K. (1989) 'Human resource management: a critical analysis'. In J. Storey (ed.) *New Perspectives in Human Resource Management*, London, Routledge.

LENGNICK-HALL, C. A. and LENGNICK-HALL, M. L. (1990) *Interactive Human Resource Management and Strategic Planning*, Westport, Quorum Books.

LIKERT, R. (1966) *New Patterns of Management*, New York, McGraw-Hill.

LOWRY, P. (1990), reported in *Personnel Management Plus*, December, p 9.

MACMILLAN, I. C. (1983) 'Seizing strategic initiative', *Journal of Business Strategy*, pp 43–57.

MARCHINGTON, M. and PARKER, P. (1990) *Changing Patterns of Employee Relations*, Hemel Hempsted, Harvester Wheatsheaf.

MARGINSON, P., EDWARDS, P. K., MARTIN, R., PURCELL, J. and SISSON, K. (1988) *Beyond the Workplace: Managing Industrial Relations in the Multi-Establishment Enterprise*, Blackwell, Oxford.

MASLOW, A. H. (1954) *Motivation and Personality*, New York, Harper & Row.

MAYO, E. (1933) *The Human Problems of an Industrial Civilisation*, London, Macmillan.

MCGREGOR, D. (1960) *The Human Side of Enterprise*, New York, McGraw-Hill.

MILLER, P. (1987) 'Strategic industrial relations and human resource management: distinction, definition and recognition', *Journal of Management Studies*, Vol. 27 No. 4, pp 347–61.

MILLER, P. (1989) 'Strategic human resource management: what it is and what it isn't, *Personnel Management*, February, pp 46–51.

MILLER, P. (1991) 'Strategic human resource management: an assessment of progress', *Human Resource Management Journal*, Vol. 1 No. 4, pp 23–39.

MINTZBERG, H. (1978) 'Patterns in strategy formation', *Management Science*, May, pp 934–48.

MINTZBERG, H. (1987) 'Crafting strategy', *Harvard Business Review*, July–August, pp 66–74.

MINTZBERG, H. (1994) 'The rise and fall of strategic planning', *Harvard Business Review*, January–February, pp 107–14.

MINTZBERG, H., QUINN, J. B. and JAMES, R. M. (1988) *The Strategy Process: Concepts, Contexts and Cases*, New York, Prentice-Hall.

MONKS, K. (1992) 'Models of personnel management: a means of understanding the diversity of personnel practices?', *Human Resource Management Journal*, Vol. 3 No. 2, pp 29–41.

MOORE, J. I. (1992) *Writers on Strategic Management*, London, Penguin Books.

NOON, M. (1992) 'HRM: a map, model or theory?' In P. Blyton and P. Turnbull (eds) *Reassessing Human Resource Management*, London, Sage Publications.

PASCALE, R. (1990) *Managing on the Edge*, London, Viking.

PASCALE, R. and ATHOS, A. (1981) *The Art of Japanese Management*, New York, Simon & Schuster.

PEACH, L. (1989) 'A practitioner's view of personnel excellence', *Personnel Management*, September, pp 37–41.

PEARCE, J. A. and ROBINSON, R. B. (1988) *Strategic Management: Strategy Formulation and Implementation*, Georgetown, Ontario, Irwin.

PERSONNEL STANDARDS LEAD BODY (1993) *A Perspective on Personnel*, London, PSLB.

PERSONNEL STANDARDS LEAD BODY (1994) *Functional Survey*, London, PSLB.

PETERS, T. (1988) *Thriving on Chaos*, Macmillan, London.

PETERS, T. and WATERMAN, R. (1982) *In Search of Excellence*, New York, Harper & Row.

PETTIGREW, A. and WHIPP, R. (1991) *Managing Change for Strategic Success*, Oxford, Blackwell.

PICKARD, J. (1993) 'From strife to plain sailing', *Personnel Management*, December, pp 38–41.

POOLE, M. (1990) 'Editorial: HRM in an international perspective', *International Journal of Human Resource Management*, Vol. 1 No. 1, pp 1–15.

PORTER, M. E. (1985) *Competitive Advantage: Creating and Sustaining Superior Performance*, New York, The Free Press.

PURCELL, J. (1988) 'The structure and function of personnel management'. In P. Marginson et al. (eds.) *Beyond the Workplace*, Oxford, Blackwell.

PURCELL, J. (1989) 'The impact of corporate strategy on human resource management'. In J. Storey (ed.) *New Perspectives on Human Resource Management*, London, Routledge.

PURCELL, J. (1993) 'The challenge of human resource management for industrial relations research and practice', *The International Journal of Human Resource Management*, Vol. 4 No. 3, pp 511–27.

PURCELL, J. (1994) 'Personnel earns a place on the board', *Personnel Management*, February, pp 26–9.

QUINN, J. B. (1980) *Strategies for Change: Logical Incrementalism*, Georgetown, Ontario, Irwin.

SISSON, K. (1990) 'Introducing the Human Resource Management Journal', *Human Resource Management Journal*, Vol. 1 No. 1, pp 1–11.

SISSON, K. (1993) 'In search of HRM', *British Journal of Industrial Relations*, Vol. 31 No. 2, pp 201–10.

SKINNER, W. (1981) 'Big hat no cattle: managing human resources', *Harvard Business Review*, 59, pp 100–4.

STACEY, R. D. (1993) 'Strategy as order emerging from chaos', *Long Range Planning*, 26(1), pp 10–17.

STARKEY K. and MCKINLEY, A. (1993) *Strategy and the Human Resource*, Oxford, Blackwell.

STOREY, J. (1987) 'Developments in the management of human resources: an interim report', *Warwick Papers on Industrial Relations*, No. 17, University of Warwick.

STOREY, J. (1989) 'From personnel management to human resource management'. In J. Storey (ed.) *New Perspectives on Human Resource Management*, London, Routledge.

STOREY, J. (1992a) *New Developments in the Management of Human Resources*, Oxford, Blackwell.

STOREY, J. (1992b) 'HRM in action: the truth is out at last', *Personnel Management*, April, pp 28–31.

STOREY, J. (1993) 'The take-up of human resource management by mainstream companies: key lessons from research', *International Journal of Human Resource Management*, Vol. 4 No. 3, pp 529–57.

STOREY, J. and SISSON, K. (1990) 'Limits to transformation: human resource management in the British context', *Industrial Relations Journal*, Vol. 21 No. 1, pp 60–5.

STREEK, W. (1987) 'The uncertainties of management in the management of uncertainty: employer, labour relations and industrial adjustment in the 1980s', *Work, Employment and Society*, Vol. 1 No. 3, pp 281–308.

THOMPSON, A. A. and STRICKLAND, A. J. (1990) *Strategic Management: Concepts and Cases*, Georgetown, Ontario, Irwin.

TORRINGTON, D. (1989) 'Human resource management and the personnel function'. In J. Storey, (ed.) *New Perspectives on Human Resource Management*, London, Routledge.

TORRINGTON, D. and HALL, L. (1991) *Personnel Management: A New Approach*, Englewood Cliffs, NJ, Prentice-Hall.

TREGOE, B. B.and ZIMMERMAN, J. W. (1980) *Top Management Strategy*, New York, Martin.

TSUI, A. S. and GOMEZ-MEJIA, L. R. (1988) 'Evaluating human resource effectiveness', in L. Dyer (ed.) *Human Resource Management: Evolving Roles and Responsibilities*, Washington DC, Bureau of National Affairs.

TYSON, S. (1985) 'Is this the very model of a modern personnel manager', *Personnel Management*, 26, pp 35–9.

TYSON, S. and FELL, A. (1986) *Evaluating the Personnel Function*, London, Hutchinson.

TYSON, S. and WITCHER, M. (1994) 'Getting in gear: post-recession HR management', *Personnel Management*, August, pp 20–3.

WALKER, J. W. (1992) *Human Resource Strategy*, New York, McGraw-Hill.

WALTON, R. E. (1985) 'From control to commitment in the workplace', *Harvard Business Review*, March–April, pp 76–84.

WHIPP, R. (1992) 'HRM: competition and strategy'. In P. Blyton and P. Turnbull (eds.) *Reassessing Human Resource Management*, London, Sage Publications.

WILKINSON, A., ALLEN, P. and SNAPE, E. (1991) 'TQM and the management of labour', *Employee Relations*, Vol. 13 No. 1, pp 24–31.

WOOLDRIDGE, B. and FLOYD, S. W. (1990) 'The strategy process, middle management involvement and organizational performance', *Strategic Management Journal*, 11, pp 231–41.

WRIGHT, P. M. and SNELL, S. A. (1989) 'Towards an integrative view of strategic human resource management', *Human Resource Management Review*, Vol. 1 No. 3, pp 203–25.

Index